FI◌

HELP ◌EM

To order more copies of this book, please call

1-866-793-9365

Charlie M◌◌◌
575-◌◌◌6574

FIGHTIN' 'EM TO HELP 'EM

BY

CHARLIE McCARTY

FRONT COVER ILLUSTRATION BY

GREM LEE

Bookstand
Publishing

www.bookstandpublishing.com

Published by
Bookstand Publishing
Morgan Hill, CA 95037
3228_4

ISBN 978-1-58909-813-8

Printed in the United States of America

CONTENTS

ONE .... INTRODUCTION 1

TWO .... THE CHURCH ON MY ROAD TO HELL 7

THREE .... RAN OUT OF TOWN (FOR PAYING MY BILLS). .. 29

FOUR .... 1981 NECESSITY AND INSPIRATION 41

FIVE .... IF YOUR TOWN GETS BEHIND YOU 51

SIX .... SUPPLIERS NEEDED 57

SEVEN .... HELP-HELP-HELP 69

EIGHT .... MY CHECK COMES WEDNESDAY 75

NINE .... GROWING PAINS 81

TEN .... PROGRESS? 93

ELEVEN .... BANNED FOR BADMOUTHING 105

TWELVE .... THE HONOR ROLL 111

THIRTEEN ...... FIGHTING MY GOVERNMENT 117

FOURTEEN ..... BOB 129

FIFTEEN .... GETTING OUT 135

EPILOGUE 147

SIXTEEN .... NEIGHBORS BY SPITE 149

SEVENTEEN ... FIGHTING IN CHURCH 161

vi

Chapter One

INTRODUCTION

"Don't leave us!"

"What'll we do without you?"

"I don't want to drive so far!

We heard those lamentations dozens of times as we held the sales to close our hardware store. But my wife and I were both well past retirement age, all efforts to sell the business had failed, and dependable hired help was impossible to keep. Not much besides liquidation of the inventory remained on our list of options.

We were tearing apart an accomplishment we had spent 27 years building in the sparsely populated mountains of Western New Mexico. The customer list had been weeded down to a mostly friendly group who paid for what they bought and depended on us to restock the shelves with what they needed. Knowing the problems our closing would create we had postponed this action as long as we could, but now with no feasible alternative in sight, we saw nothing else to do but sell the stock and close the door. We'd remember that those customers who came back time after time and paid their bills were really the ones who kept it open.

All memories, however, weren't pleasant. All customers weren't good. Most of the 27 years had been a fight with individuals who wanted the convenience of anything they needed in a store near their homes. But they wanted it at the price they'd pay in the big stores two hundred miles away. Those conflicts caused us to wake up each morning asking ourselves, "How did we get into this mess?"

I'll answer that question by starting this story about fifty years ago. Most of my life I've had to fight with someone I was trying to help. That started with the U.S. Forest Service. My first book, *Trouble in a Green Pickup*, is a detailed account of that battle. I was running ranches that didn't pay their own way and had to make my living somewhere else. Carpenter work paid the bills for about twenty years.

But the materials and supplies were around Albuquerque, a long hard day in a slow truck to get to most of the things we needed. This led me to stockpiling a few leftovers and common necessities in an old hay barn. My neighbors learned they might come to my place and get what they needed for their own jobs. I considered it absolutely necessary to always be a good neighbor.

Their demands expanded faster than I could accommodate them. They came whether I had the money, the time or the storage space to fill their requirements. If a man got a few pieces of lumber he'd also tell me he needed nails, paint, and a new hammer handle.

The challenge got out of hand. We couldn't help them all, but we tried. One neighbor was so persistent he became a nuisance who dug through my plywood scrap so many times he knew each piece better than I. "I saw it here last week" and he'd pull it out of the bottom of the pile. He seldom offered any money, saying, "If you ever need anything—come and see if you can find it at my place." That would have been wasted effort as he owned nothing but some badly worn and patched farm equipment. Yet he had a knack for making me feel obligated to keep helping. That occurred one day after I'd spent about twelve hours sitting in an old, worn out, flatbed truck to bring home 100 sacks of cement. Five minutes after I crawled out of the cab he was in my yard, hauling a cow of mine that had gotten on the wrong side of our fence, "Oh, I'm glad to see that! I need a sack!" He took a bag off my load and carried it to the passenger's seat of his pickup before unloading the cow or finding out if I'd sell any. "How much did you pay for it?" He asked as an afterthought.

"Four dollars and sixty-five cents," I told him, "and all day in that truck. And $100.00 through the gas tank."

Most neighbors who gladly took care of each other's stock would have been deeply offended at any mention of payment for such service. I'd taken his cattle back home lots of times.

He got defensive real fast. "I didn't charge you for bringing your cow home! And she didn't just climb in my pickup! I had to saddle my horse and put her in the corral."

When it became obvious I wasn't going to give him the cement he fumbled through his pants pockets, his shirt, his jacket and

2

then the ash tray of his pickup before finding $3.49. "If that cow ain't worth the difference, I'll buy 'er from ya." He was obviously unhappy.

As a gesture of friendship I let him have the cement. A few days passed and he was back, wanting ten sacks. I'd used my load. He said, "Let me know when you're going back for more. You can get me some."

Then I found a gate thrown open in our fence as if he was working on paying in advance for the next order. I must have had "stupid" stenciled across the middle of my face when I let him have that first sack.

I led myself into a trap. I couldn't stay with the family ranch without money from some other source. Carpenter work had been a good supplement. But everywhere I turned I was under attack from some politician or bureaucrat who wanted to tax, harass or eliminate me.

Trouble in a Green Pickup was written to track the effects of a mad politician seeking vengeance against our Western livestock industry. President Lyndon B. Johnson retaliated for the way we had voted at the end of his term in office. His grazing fee increase became a loaded gun that is still aimed at us over forty years later.

I was determined to stay with that ranch though I'd have to pay the government so much for the use of their forage, I'd have to raise money from another source to survive. We owned a little over twelve hundred acres of mountain stream bottom that was mixed with twenty thousand acres of National Forest. No fences separated them. The legal boundaries were a checkerboard arrangement of quarter-mile zigzags along bluffs and steep mountainsides. These homesteads dated back to the 1880's when the government used free land as bait to draw settlers into the West.

Those pioneers usually couldn't make a living on the 160 acres the government awarded them for building a home, cultivating some ground and managing to hold out three years. Grazing permits on the adjacent National Forest land were the band-aid, the reward for perseverance that the government gave the survivors. Political favoritism entered the picture. Some ranchers received permits for hundreds of head of livestock—others only a few. Those who didn't get

3

sizable numbers in grazing permits sold to neighbors or abandoned their claims and moved on to more lucrative jobs in the cities. A nominal fee was to be paid to the government to cover the administrative costs of the permits. The bureaucrats hired assistants and assistants for the assistants. They catered to demands of people in the cities who wanted all this federal land set aside as a preserve or national park. By Johnson's time they confused a grazing permit with a lease and thought we should pay a rate similar to what was charged for irrigated cropland.

Since 1883 my family had been tough, tenacious and stubborn. They worked hard and made every dollar count as smaller ranches failed. They paid off tax liens, bank foreclosures and made purchases from disgruntled heirs. My family managed both the private and public land as one ranch unit because fences along the legal boundaries would have made an unworkable mess of the whole place.

Those twelve hundred acres along the streams were the most level and fertile, produced the best forage and furnished the only dependable surface water for miles. But because the private land was not fenced separate the Forest Service governed it the same as their own and allowed a credit of only fifteen head of cattle we could run without paying grazing fees.

Land values had risen tremendously by the time Dad died and I took over the management of the ranch. People on the street were jealous and chided me that I inherited instant wealth. They didn't look close enough to see I'd really taken a very low-paying job. My mother retained her ownership and control for the next thirty years. I was not allowed to sell or mortgage a thing. I kept her and my three younger siblings supplied with beef, milk, butter, eggs and garden vegetables. They stayed warm through all the winters with firewood I cut and hauled then they rewarded me with the constant complaint, "I never got anything out of the ranch."

I got married at age twenty, adding Thelma, as helpmate who joined me in my assignments, chores and duties. She brought in outside money for our living expenses with waitress jobs in a café, as a clerk in the post office or cook in the school cafeteria. As our three children joined the family it became difficult for her to make enough at those jobs to pay the baby sitter. She started staying at home, reupholstering old furniture.

We struggled, provided for ourselves, helped neighbors and moved forward as my family had lived for nearly a hundred years. We would have liked to have had more friends. But that family owned land seemed to constantly be an obstacle, a barrier to congeniality. It was only a bunch of dirt, rocks, brush and home to fifteen cows; something that appeared on the tax rolls to make payments on the new schoolhouses—but a cause for envy from the people who had to pay thousands of dollars for a vacant lot so they could park a house trailer. It was a reason for a mechanic or doctor to bill us for twice as much as they charged any of our neighbors and a cause for heckling and taunts anytime we came close to the town busybodies who couldn't mind their own business.

They gossiped and spread rumors about us from the coffee shops, despised us in the government offices and if there was a bully among their kids, he picked fights with ours on the schoolyard. But they all came on the run with smiles on their faces if we owned something they wanted to borrow.

The following stories chronicle the use and abuse we experienced as a result of trying to be helpful neighbors and provide services that were needed in our remote community.

As much as possible I've left out or disguised the names of the people involved. I'd like to leave a record of our struggles without making it an attack on those good people. They had their justification to support their actions and attitudes—as I had reasons for mine. It would cheapen this work and make it unacceptable if I used fictitious names.

I hope it comes through as what I've intended, interesting non-fiction.

Chapter Two

THE CHURCH ON MY ROAD TO HELL

The middle 1970's found me taking any part-time job I could find to support my wife and three young kids. I was determined to make a living close to home while finding time to run a ranch that wasn't paying its own way—like everyone else who owned one of the ranches where cattle graze National Forest Land, we were forced into another job or occupation if we paid our bills. That business raising a calf from the time it is born until it is weaned is one that is easy to fall in love with, become addicted to and make a man dig his own grave to keep him from leaving.

I was the third generation of the same family to run the operation my grandfather had started in the 1880's. He'd survived threats from renegade Indians, droughts, blizzards, and the isolation of having to take a horse-drawn wagon for a one-hundred mile trip to Magdalena when he had to buy supplies. He endured trips through scorching heat with no available water, a bout of blindness from sun glare on drifts of snow and many overnight camps with no protection from the wind. Surely, if he could make it through those times and the First World War, a flu epidemic and the Great Depression, I could find a way to hang on to the place and keep going.

My father had taken over part of Granddad's ranch toward the end of that Great Depression and continued almost without help through the manpower shortage of the Second World War. He was constantly building improvements when I joined the family and they started assigning me jobs as soon as I learned to walk. My first lessons were to stretch every dollar to the limit, and to make maximum productive use of every moment of our time.

Making a living meant growing everything we ate. If spring frosts held off and spared the blossoms on the apple trees we were promised a luxury, a treat to guard, protect and try to consume every bite. That meant trimming out any bird or worm damage, cut away the bruises from the windfalls and carry the waste to the chickens or hogs. We'd carefully select all the fruit that had no blemish, wrap each individual apple in old newspaper and store it in the cool dark cellar for fresh eating or pies through the winter. We were now reaping rewards from my grandmother's labor. She had planted an orchard as seedlings, carried water in a bucket or irrigated from a hand-dug ditch because she was driven by the desire to raise fruit in her own backyard. There were other stories about how the whole family took the wagon and team forty miles to Glenwood, camped along the way, and picked fruit for half the crop. They also owned a hand cranked cider press, currently displayed in my store--for squeezing their own juice when the trees produced an abundance of fruit. But in order to keep up with changing times the things that were held dear by one generation became obsolete for the next. Now I was in a scene in which the economics of ranching forced me to waste the fruit because I couldn't leave my job. No local resident would pick it for half; they wouldn't even pick it if it was free. Their families wouldn't go hungry if they didn't want to work because they were assured they could buy groceries with food stamps.

So my most valuable inheritance was not land or cattle; it was the habit and tradition of self-reliance. Whatever we wanted or gained in material possessions, we got through hard work and determination. The only way I could protect the footholds that came to me from the generations before me would be through starting my own business or taking on additional jobs.

I would owe it to any potential employer to be on the job on time and give my undivided attention to whatever he wanted me to do. This left no way to be gone because a cow needed help giving birth to her calf or bringing her back home after she had crossed to the wrong side of a fence. All roads seemed to lead me into my own business, selling a necessary product or providing some service for the other people in my area.

I scrounged through junk piles and put together an old truck which brought in a few dollars as I used it to haul cattle to the sales for my neighbors. Then I started building a home which drove me into debt for the lumber. Several months passed in which I made no progress at making a payment so I offered to take a sawmill job and trade labor for what I owed.

Stanley Shumway, who ran the sawmill, thought if I owed him for lumber I should know something about carpentry. He wanted to build two homes and put me on as a carpenter's helper. It was an unexpected turn of events that set my course for the next twenty years.

The boss who I was supposed to be assisting never appeared at the job. Shumway wasn't going to let a man stand idle so he started me preparing ground then laying a foundation. He sent me helpers who knew less than I and told me to keep them busy. He bawled me out every time I made a false move, told me I was too slow, but kept me working. Eventually a sturdy house appeared on his ground, constructed completely with untrained help and out of cull material he couldn't sell from his mill. He started me on a second home, still watching every penny and we came to a parting of the ways by the time the roof went on. This was early 1960's when a comfortable three bedroom home could be completed for around $10,000.00. He said I'd spent $2,500.00 getting that two bedroom job to the dried-in stage. He thought that was exorbitant and fired me but our town had watched me work and decided I was a carpenter.

Now I could make my living with a claw hammer but that beginning placed me in a niche with customers who wanted everything fast and cheap. Never climbing out of that hole, other builders got the high-dollar top quality jobs. I made sure my work was level, square and stout which brought on daily fights with clients who thought I was supposed to nail together their projects without so much accuracy as the use of a measuring tape.

About this time the church where I'd spent my youth burned to the ground. I'd been so busy with the pressures of making a living that I'd drifted away from church work but Thelma and I had three young kids who I was anxious to get started. I was doing all I could to influence them in proper honesty and morals and assumed it would come easier if they could get a firm foundation in knowledge and application of the Bible.

This was the second time in my lifetime the Community church had been destroyed by fire. Several years went by in which services were held in an abandoned school house twelve miles away at Apache Creek. They conducted no classes for children—the preacher's excuse—"I can't do anything, I don't have a building." He made it clear he was hired to preach, not build, and "If the Lord wants me to have a church he'll provide it."

There were discussions of rebuilding on the old foundation but a street widening project had left them without parking space and a steep climb to get to the entry steps. A person needed considerable athletic ability to get to the front door.

Lumber, log and masonry were all considered as the new building was discussed—lots of talk but no progress.

Some combination of donated funds and insurance money let them purchase a prefabricated metal building which they unloaded on land that Emil Kiehne donated. The building salesman convinced the preacher, "It is like an "Erector" set. Your congregation can bolt it together." He thought they would meet and work in peace and harmony and soon have their nice new building.

I told the preacher he was overlooking several important steps. A floor plan had to be drawn. The ground had to be leveled and compacted. The plumbing had to be installed. A square and level floor and foundation had to be in place before any assembly could start.

He listened with a look of total indifference. "We have a building committee. We're going to let them decide. It's not my job!" Another time he told me, "You've had one preacher who dug a basement with a wheelbarrow. It won't be me!" He was referring to Roger Sherman, a cowboy type preacher who was not afraid to get his hands dirty.

This situation caused the preacher and several members of the congregation to tell me "You're the only one that understands all that. You should donate it."

"I've always worked with lumber." I tried to argue. "Prefabricated steel is new to me."

Their answer was, "I'll bet you can figure it out."

I told them "It's too big a job to donate. I'm taking the building jobs because my cattle aren't making me a living."

Two years went by with part numbers fading in the weather and people playing with the small loose parts. There was nothing to keep someone from making their own use of bundles of rods and bolts. I did a lot of soul searching in those two years. We were self-reliant people in a self-reliant town. We'd always taken care of our needs by growing our own food. Our homes had always been a shelter we put together ourselves from materials we could gather with our own hands. My parent's generation had built their own schools. I was going to have to find the time to do my part if my kids got the chance to get any religious training.

I misled myself with very fond memories from church work during my own adolescence. I hadn't yet learned that all preachers aren't leaders.

Between 1947 and 1954, as I grew from age seven to fourteen, the pastor was Bill Lytle who covered a lot of ground. Glenwood was on the south and Fence Lake at the north tip of a 300 mile drive he had to make on Sundays. Back then not an inch of paved road existed. Once a month he also preached at the Whiting Sawmill at Collins Park. This was on the opposite side of Eagle Peak, fifty miles of rough road to get twenty airline miles east of Reserve.

Every person on that route was important to Reverend Lytle. He knew who was sick or hungry and organized help where it was needed. He reached out to people who were not members of his church while refereeing the basketball games. He even got my Dad to go to church.

Dad didn't have any objection to churches. He'd just spent his life where there weren't any. He might lose his temper and say words he shouldn't, but he lived his life helping his neighbors and no one questioned his honesty. It really made mom happy when he sometimes put down his tools on a Sunday morning to go to church.

Mr. Lytle found a way to involve every kid in town. When he gave a lesson from Matt. 25, 14-27, the parable of the talents, he handed each of the young people a dollar bill, a fortune to most of us. His instructions were, "This is seed money. Put it to work. Spend it in some way that makes more money. When you come back next week you can show me what you did with it."

Some of the kids spent their bonanza on candy or toys and didn't return. The girls pooled theirs, purchased flour, sugar, chocolate and made a few dollars selling home-made baked goodies. One of my buddies talked his dad into letting him use an old pickup. We boys spent our dollars on gasoline, and went around the town cleaning backyards and emptying trash barrels. The results were the direct application of a Bible lesson, a successful fund raising project, a town cleanup, and finding productive uses for teenage energy. I always thought that lesson could be projected to mean it is not illegal or immoral to make a profit if you are using your money for honorable intentions.

That preacher led the kids of Catron and surrounding counties through summer camps, hayrides and Christmas carols. Whole communities turned out for Sunday afternoon picnics and a softball game.

A mason who lived across the street from the church had two ragged little boys who got into mischief all over town. Some people were offended to see them attend because they were so dirty. Mr. Lytle decided we needed a neat white cross set in concrete at the back of the parking lot. He strung out the project through a week of Vacation Bible School and kept those kids coming every day because he'd convinced them we needed their expertise mixing concrete.

When Reverend Lytle moved on he left a void that has never been filed. With no leadership and the distractions I found to accompany my own adolescence it was easy for me to drift away from the church. Before I left, however, I witnessed an incident involving the wife of the next man who spoke from that pulpit; I believe it played a direct part in sending one young man down the wrong road. Jess and Alice Brennand were raising an adopted son on their ranch. As the crow flies they were about fifteen miles from town, but the series of Forest Service roads and abandoned logging trails added up to around eighty miles of vehicle torture to get there.

Jess was a helpful neighbor but gruff, boisterous and rough talking. They home-schooled the little boy so he had no contact with other kids and was growing up to sound just like his dad.

A temporary logging road was built through the Negrito Creek. Now when the weather was good the Brennands were about and hour from town. I frequently had to go to their place to bring home cattle that had crossed the fence and remember sitting at their table, drinking coffee, while Alice told me this story. "I was thrilled when we got that road. Now we could get our mail every week. Stores and doctors were closer, and I even thought I could get Bill into the kids

Bible School. So I got up early one Sunday and gave him a bath. I put on my best dress and a pair of stockings. But it had rained all night. That red clay on the mesa before you drop off the hill to the Russ Place was slick and my pickup slid into the ditch. I had to get out and put on tire chains. When I got back on the road I had to take them off."

I'd been in church that Sunday so I knew the rest of the story. Halfway through the services we heard the back door open. The preacher's wife was the first to turn around. She was the type that considered it necessary for everyone who entered the Sanctuary to be primped and polished to perfection, and when she screamed an "e-e-e-k." everyone turned to look.

There stood Alice and Bill Brennand, mud-splattered and humiliated to tears. They never came back. As he grew up, little Bill fell in with the wrong crowd. He was arrested and jailed several times on drug-related charges.

Knowing some of the good as well as the bad influence a church could have on young people, and wanting my kids to be trained as I had been, I let myself be lead into a pilot's position. I'd been raised in a do-it yourself philosophy. My parents and grandparents had built their own roads, schoolhouses and churches. Volunteer muscle power was the substitute for non-existent cash. I'd try to steer them straight and put that building together for a minimal cost. I thought the more help they gave me the less time I'd bill them for.

They distorted my plan to, "Let's do all we can when Charlie isn't here. That way we won't have to pay him."

Some of the group wanted to hire a contractor, a turn-key job to put the building together. They couldn't put their hands on enough money to get one interested.

"Just get something started." The preacher urged me. "If people can see we are doing something they will start contributing." I had to schedule my work to avoid conflicts with ranch needs, especially shipping season in September and October. This meant it was necessary to finish the site preparation and concrete work ahead of freezing weather. I could come back later for the assembly portion.

The first step would be getting the ground ready.

At that time the County Commissioners were very liberal with the use of their men and machinery. Anyone could get the use of a road grader, a loader, a dump truck, and their operators if they'd remember where the help came from the next time they voted. A church group could be an important block at election time. The preacher had no trouble getting help.

"Let me know when the grader can be there." I told him, "I'll go up there with a transit and set some grade stakes to help him get the ground level." He acted completely indifferent.

A few weeks passed, the preacher came to me with, "The ground is level. You can start building." He gave me a blank stare when I asked if anyone had checked the level with an instrument. The weeds had been scraped away leaving bare ground but any place I tried to set his 60x60 foot building there were two feet of slope from the highest corner to the lowest. The equipment had been sent to a different part of the county and wouldn't be back for a month.

I told the preacher, "You're going to have to get someone who knows what he is doing to take charge of this job. He needs to have the personality of a drill sergeant. If you don't get organized you're going to have a mess. It is absolutely necessary to get the foundation square and level."

The preacher's vision was still something that would be put together in a weekend. He enjoyed prowling through garage sales and flea markets so he got busy looking for bargains in finish material. Borrowing my truck several times, he soon stuffed several local garages and store rooms with part-sheets of plywood and scraps of drywall.

Unconcerned when I insisted on quality work, he answered with, "I don't care." Then he prepared a sermon, complete with scripture references directed at me. The theme was "Good works won't save you."

I used what I had, a front loader on a farm tractor to get the site ready. Sometimes I could get the preacher to hold the surveyor's rod when I checked grade. He strained my patience with his lack of knowledge and interest. I had to show him at every shot how standing behind the rod instead of beside it would get it in a vertical position for an accurate reading. Then just as often I had to tell him, "I need to read the face, not the back," or "Don't turn it upside down!"

The job would become very lonesome if they could talk me into donating my time, so I decided I'd work for half price. At that time I was charging other customers around ten dollars an hour. If they got me and my tools for five they were getting a bargain. Working for a small fee should be an incentive for some of them to come and help me. A little money coming into my account would ease some of the strain on our personal budget.

Those who had encouraged me with "I bet you can figure it out" soon complained "You don't know what you are doing!"

Those who had said, "Get something started. The money will start coming," now said "I'm not giving anything if Charlie's getting it!"

My strongest opposition came from another rancher who complained, "Charlie has more cows than I do. I'm not making any money from mine but I'm not asking the church to help me!"

Then he asked, "Why should I work for free if he's getting paid?"

The group became sharply divided in a committee meeting. Some wanted floors covered with tile while others held out for carpet. Tile would be easy to clean. Carpet would silence the noise of people moving. These were finishing details that were irrelevant at the start of the job. The preacher wanted to keep his flock together. His safest tactic was to join them in attacking every move I made.

My only friendly encouragement came to me from one man, Julius Willamson, a retired school teacher who claimed no knowledge of construction. He came every day, never argued or got in the way, kept his mind on his business and tried to think ahead. Very often when I needed a tool he had it in his hand. His wife, Marie, was just as supportive. She often brought hot or cold drinks, and home-made goodies.

When the ground was level, I improvised compaction equipment by having a loaded dump truck spend a day driving back and forth in each direction to get a firm base below the slab.

Someone borrowed a chain trencher attached to a tractor to dig the ditches for the footings. It could claw its way forward without an operator, so he walked away and left no one to guide it. It veered away from my marks. Then he took the machine home. No one volunteered to help the day I had to use a pick and shovel to put the trench where it was supposed to be.

A retired plumber glanced at the plan to get a general location of the restrooms and started digging with a backhoe.

"You'd better do something to get square." I told him.

"That's square!" He hadn't even used a measuring tape.

His crooked result gave me no place to put the plumbing wall without having vent pipes exposed in one of the bathrooms. The deviation from square lines was going to be obvious when the time came to install floor or ceiling tiles.

To make the form building simple I decided to pour the concrete footing and floor in two stages with blocked out spaces where the main support columns and anchor bolts would go. Then I drove rebar grade stakes to a level that was four inches below the plan for the finished floor.

We needed to avoid delays. Summer was gone. But some of the people who promised to help refused to interrupt their vacation plans. We also had to avoid the county fair and Labor Day weekend. I had to bend my schedule to fit what they wanted to do.

J. T. Hollimon hauled a pile of gravel. Hugh B. McKeen furnished an old mixer truck. We finally got a community workday and poured the footings. I'd stayed there longer than I should. I hoped the weather would stay warm and we could get back for the floor after my calves were sold.

While I was gone to work cattle the preacher and the plumber decided to install heating ducts below the floor. They bluntly informed me, "We don't need you."

Destroying my leveling and compaction, they dug ditches and buried large cardboard tubes in concrete. On one side they came out over two inches above my floor grade. The only way I could cover that bump was by raising the whole job. Their carelessness increased the concrete we needed, added to the fill dirt and wasted days of time.

They tore down the batter boards I'd left to locate the outside lines of the building. The clean footings were lost under loose dirt piles and they paid no attention to my grade stakes. I had to re-design the floor to fit the mess they'd left. It was tempting to quit. But I could see the job never getting done if I didn't take the lead. I wanted to chew out the whole crew but I couldn't muster a vocabulary that was appropriate near a church.

When the preacher and one of his elders stopped to talk about something totally irrelevant, standing where they were blocking my view and drowning out communication between me, at the transit, and whoever was holding the surveyors rod. I emphatically told them to "Shut up and get out of my way!" I was going to have to be the drill sergeant.

The volunteer help didn't materialize. They were men who had made it to retirement age wearing business suits and neckties. It was unthinkable to expect them to operate shovels and wheelbarrows. The younger ones had to be at their jobs and support their families. They would never find enough free time to get this done.

One old man promised to decorate the windows with stained glass when we got around to putting up the walls. He drove his car into the middle of the job and bawled me out for my slow progress. The dump truck driver didn't see him, backed up and smashed his grille and radiator. Now the County Government, which had been trying to help, had to process the liability claim he filed against them for his damaged automobile.

One man was accustomed to doing a hard day's work and had lots of free time. His wife's job provided their livelihood. He could have been good help but found more pleasure and amusement when he was keeping an argument going. That appeared to be his prime motive for coming to the job. He never missed an opportunity to bicker, growl and scowl--then proceed in the wrong way to go about whatever he was doing. He was the most vehement in opposing any pay for my services. If he'd been on a payroll it would have been very simple to fire him and send him home—even though we were begging for help. I didn't have the authority or luxury to dismiss anyone. I sure couldn't run anyone out of a church. Privately I named him "Screw Up" and tolerated his interference. He took the lead and set a pace which the preacher seemed to enjoy following.

It was usually ten o'clock in the morning before any helpers appeared. None carried a lunch. They drifted back and forth to check their mail, go to the bank, or run family errands. It was like a baby sitting job. One guy dismantled one of my power tools to see what made it work. I told them this job would stop if they couldn't get me some dependable help.

A steady stream of hippies came through town. The Rainbow Family held an encampment nearby and Catron County gained a reputation for being the easiest place in the nation to get on welfare. They were dressed in rags and never combed their hair. Some were barefoot. The smell of marijuana only half masked the odor of their unwashed bodies; they were young and some could do a day's work. That was all the help I could get and the church willingly paid them more than they were paying me. Now I had a carpenter crew with no one who could read a measuring tape. They thought a level or square took too much time and if I told one to put a mark on a board he had to borrow a pencil. If he broke the lead he needed my knife. This project was supposed to benefit the local community but license plates from West Virginia, Idaho and California appeared where they parked their cars.

When the time came to pour the floor I insisted they get someone who knew something about concrete. Any lack of help or an equipment breakdown could result in an error that would be in place for a very long time. They let me hire Don Kinsman. He was experienced, had the equipment and made it clear he had no intention of doing anything that could be construed as helping a church. He was so vague about his charges I was uneasy they might not have the money to pay him.

Running a jerry-rigged operation, we used front loaders to pick up gravel and bagged cement to fill the mixer truck. Men had to stand on a precarious footing ten feet in the air to break the sacks. The town water system was too slow to get it in the mix, so we had to run it through a metal stock tank and a pump that was powered by a cantankerous Briggs and Stratton engine. The mixing process took time. One batch would be getting stiff before another was ready to dump.

I'd spread the word we shouldn't stop for lunch. The women got together and made sandwiches, but some of the crew found time to smoke marijuana. They provided our afternoon entertainment, a drug-charged hippie singing and tap dancing from the top of the rolling drum of a concrete truck.

I smelled smoke. The man who only came to screw up had stacked the empty cement bags and built a bonfire a few feet from the back of my pickup. Flames blew toward a five-gallon can of extra gasoline near the tailgate.

I hollered at the preacher. "Move that pickup! The keys are in it!"

The preacher decided to run some errand downtown. He failed to notice that my pickup, which had a pipe stock rack for hauling horses, was leaving with the tailgate unlatched. It was swinging and banging four feet out to the right hand side.

I yelled at someone else. "Hey stop that preacher! That gate will get someone's windshield!"

Someone saw humor in the situation, "I really don't think he'll hurt the tailgate.

The Lord had to have been watching over that crew. We got through the day without killing anyone.

The sun was low when the last batch was dumped. Those of us who had fought concrete all day were exhausted. The volunteers went home. The preacher and the Screw-Up went to their homes too. We'd get the rest of the day without interruption from them. Clouds spitting sleet and snow blew in on a cold wind. A slow miserable wait

19

was coming before the concrete would be ready to finish. Don Kinsman informed me he'd go home if I didn't get some good wood and build a bonfire to keep us warm. He also demanded a little refreshment to ease the pain while we were waiting.

"Start with a couple of pints of good bourbon and a case of beer." He told me.

I complied, knowing I could stand a few nips myself. The church was christened with liquid spirits and Kinsman informed me he wouldn't be around for any housewarming celebration.

A couple of the hippies stayed on the job. They were accustomed to late-night parties and they had their own supply of painkiller.

When the concrete was stiff enough for the power trowel we had to start another cold and balky air-cooled engine. I learned to hate and distrust those things with a passion.

There were two or three repetitious days of the concrete pouring scene. Added yardage resulted from having to raise the floor to get above the duct work. We ran out of gravel. The trucks that had brought our first pile weren't available. All we could do was borrow a dump truck and go to a nearby arroyo.

The slab finally got finished. It became my job to study the drawings and make sure each piece of steel was bolted in the right place. The preacher brought a bunch of men he'd found in a coffee shop and told me, "These guys know what they are doing. They'll get it done in a few days."

One of them was cocky. "We don't have to waste our time studying drawings. Use a little common sense. Those big posts hold it up; Those I-beams go across the building. The red iron is the frame. The short sheets of metal are the sides. The long ones are the roof!"

I would have been glad to get off the job but I wondered how that preacher had the nerve to quibble and contest every dollar I'd spent, and then offer to turn the task over to strangers at the moment he'd planned when he could bring the community together and work in a joint effort.

I'd studied the drawings. I told them, "Four of those posts have holes for the center bay rod bracing. The holes in two match the east end hardware. The west wall is completely different. It can be removed if they want to expand. You can't get all that right without looking at the blueprints!"

They argued, "If a hole's missing we'll burn one with a torch."

I gained no favor with the preacher, but they didn't come back trying to take over the job.

A sewer line contactor had brought a crane to town and we arranged to get the use of it to stand up the heavy structural steel. The skeleton outline set off explosive criticism that stopped the job. Now obvious it was going to have a flat roof, everyone seemed to think churches should be tall and steep. The preacher shrugged it off with, "Charlie's doing it. We're stuck with whatever he gives us."

I told them, "I didn't design it and I didn't build it! I'm pulling the parts out of the pile, finding the right place to put each one and putting the bolts in them! Any changes in design should have been before the building was ordered!"

"We don't have to accept it! We can change it!" Some of them had talked to a welder. "We can get some metal from old truck frames. It's stout. We can make some extensions that will make the roof steeper, now's the time to do it before you make a bigger mess!" They drew some quick sketches of what they had in mind.

"You're the ones that'll be making the mess!" I didn't try to control my temper. "If you change the angle at the peak, you'll have to change it at the top of the walls! You'll make the roof metal come out too short and no part of the end walls will fit!"

The preacher said, "I told you we'll have to take whatever Charlie gives us." I needed to use a telephone so I went to the nearest house to borrow Clara Snyder's. She was a very frail elderly woman who had been watching every move. In a shaking voice she said, "Charlie, I taught you in your first Sunday School. You're going to make us a new church."

They all knew I was close to walking away.

Julius Williamson was close to tears. "We can't get it done without you." He and his wife were the only ones still part of the job that weren't mad at me. But the real driving force was the three little kids I had at home. I wanted to see them get their chance to go to Sunday school.

A weekend was scheduled to use as much help as they could get to assemble the sidewall and roof purlins. One wooden crate held over a ton of clips and braces. Each was identified by part numbers on the drawings; a mass of confusion I had to translate to understandable instructions like East or West, and roof or wall. Then I'd figure out which side went up and how to turn each part.

Knowing the limitations of my crew I started that day at the crack of dawn, putting each type of part in a pile near the part of the building where it would be used. When the Screw-Up got to the job he immediately started carrying my piles to the opposite end of the building and telling everyone. "I think it looks better over here." The preacher joined him in laughter thinking it was funny.

That was a Saturday. The next day they decided to worship at the job. The preacher prepared a message that would be a pep talk. A considerable part was devoted to the need for more contributions to keep things moving. To stand above the crowd he leaned a ladder against the framework and spoke from the third rung. He presented a comical appearance. That ladder had a distinct taper from bottom to top and he'd turned it upside down. I snickered and moved to the back to avoid interrupting him as he asked everyone to join him. "We'll get this done!" He told them. "I've built lots of churches."

Every day we battled insufficient funds and lack of interest. The hippie crew moved out of town, leaving me with volunteer help who came or left as they pleased. I started each morning not knowing if I'd have any help or how difficult they would try to make my job when they got there.

Progress was slower than a snail's pace. Some times they had the money to pay me and there were times they told me I'd have to wait. I took other jobs as they became available which caused complaints, "He just works for us when he wants to." Others who had more Bible knowledge quoted chapter and verse when they told me, "Your first obligation is to the Lord. His work should come first."

When we reached the point we were putting siding on the north sidewall the man who was going to put the stained glass on the windows informed me he wanted the building all to himself for a few months. He had been one of my most vocal opponents every other time something caused a delay. Now he wanted space to lay each window flat on sawhorses while he took the time to work with small pieces of colored glass. Years had passed during which that arrangement could have been made in anyone's garage.

"I don't want to stop right now." I told him. Then I asked, "Do you think you can leave your work exposed, in an open building, and no one will mess with it?"

"They should be proud to get it," he argued.

"Don't think for a minute this town thinks this is holy ground." I answered. "It is common for me to have to clean up empty beer cans, or broken wine bottles when I get here in the morning. There was even one time that a hammer was left out overnight. Someone stretched a spent condom over the handle."

Those windows were never covered with stained glass. I hadn't let his plan cause delay so more people were upset with the way I was running the job.

When the outside was finished, all the prefabricated steel was in place and we were on our own to design whatever went on the inside.

The local sawmill company donated the lumber for the interior frame work. Wood paneling was planned for inside finish. I spent a lot of time studying how to frame around a sidewall girt that ran completely around the building seven feet off the floor at the top of all the doors and windows. They were talking about a nine-foot ceiling in the main sanctuary and eight for the classrooms and hallways.

My worry was that if I split the framework to go over and under that girt I was designing slow carpenter work. If I moved out in front of it I was wasting a foot of space all the way around the building.

As usual when I solicited an opinion from some of them I got an answer that was so stupid it was comical. "Just put the ceiling line at that iron thing," they told me. "That's high enough."

"Well, you want a raised platform for the speaker." I answered. "I'll have to cut a hole in the ceiling so a tall man can talk into the attic." They let me take the time to frame over and under the girt.

They split my count for the paneling order, deciding to use a gray color in the sanctuary and brown in the hall and classrooms. The preacher and the Screw-Up had a field day carrying scraps to wrong rooms and trying to mix both colors on the same wall. The job had turned into a fight for every board. They tried to run the stripes horizontal instead of vertical. To further aggravate me they nailed some with the finished side hidden, a bare side exposed to view. Then the real fight came over the foot of extra height in the sanctuary. I showed them that every panel had the same pattern of light and dark lines, resembling a rough-lumber finish. If we installed each sheet with the narrowest stripe on the left the top and bottom rows would match.

"Why can't we put narrow on the right?"

"That will work too but we'll have to check it at every sheet. I'd like to pick one pattern and stay with it. I'll measure and cut, you guys can nail. We'll know what each other is doing!"

I was expecting too much when I tried to get any cooperation from those two. You can go into that sanctuary today and see two places where they broke the pattern. The foot that was spliced at the top doesn't match the sheet below it.

Irregularities in the floor showed up at the top of the walls. I wanted a narrow band of trim molding around the room to cover that splice. The preacher wanted to save money. When I wasn't around he ripped some scrap paneling into strips and nailed it in place. Part of the time he ran it with vertical lines, part horizontal and some from gray scrap and other from brown. Then he mixed in strips of white from the ceiling tile. Only someone who knew how he had worked to aggravate me through the whole job could appreciate the mess he'd made. I let it hang until the rest of the building was ready for molding. Then I ripped it down, threw it in the trash and did the job the way it should have been done.

The next episode in the daily battle with the preacher came when he returned from one of his trips to a yard sale carrying a used toilet from a recreation vehicle. This one had a built-in water pump with wires dangling for an electrical connection. "Can you use this? I got it cheap."

"It's a piece of junk in my way!" I told him.

I'd hurt his feelings. He sat it down beside where I was working and disappeared. For several days he made sure it followed me wherever I was working-- classrooms, hallway, kitchen or office. A day came that I was working on the raised platform where the podium would be. I carried it to center stage and firmly fastened it to the floor with two long screws.

A bunch of women appeared touring their new building. So they wouldn't notice my laughing, I found something to do in another room. There was a blood-curdling scream—a pause—and a terrified feminine voice saying, "I hope that's not a permanent fixture."

That was the last I saw of the preacher's electric toilet.

He kept on with his efforts to raise money. To get around the people who were "Not going to put in a dime if Charlie's getting any of it," he started one account to buy pews and another to purchase song books. A little brass tag would be placed on the pew or a paper tag glued in the front of the song book permanently recognizing the contributor.

I hadn't turned in my time records for two months because they'd told me they didn't have any money. I didn't want my name attached to anything around the place. I definitely didn't want my opponents to claim victory. Getting my services for nothing had been their goal from the start. Telling no one, I tore up those records long before finishing the job

Showing them where someone else could do part of the work, I suggested the women stain the molding. They might be more particular than the men. I set up sawhorses, and let them have it.

Thinking I'd use whatever they gave me, I insisted they do this ahead of laying the floor though I knew none would credit me with any wisdom. They got more stain on the floor and sawhorses than the molding. Someone did a perfect job on the hidden side while missing the face and edges. No one bothered to clean a paint brush. But with only minimal time lost to touch-up, that detail was out of the way.

Glue is supposed to go down first and then the floor tile. Whoever took the lead on that job must have thought it best to change that order—at least that is the way the job appeared. In places glue was splattered a foot above the floor on the wall paneling. They stopped the tile six inches away from some of the walls, cleaned no tools and left the lid off several half-empty cans of adhesive.

Tired of trying to get any of them to do anything right, I told the preacher, "If these smears get cleaned up, someone else is going to do it. And a bunch of the baseboards the ladies have stained are going to be wasted. I need a load of old railroad ties to cover the edges they skipped!"

Someone else's elbow grease cleaned up the mess. They may have rented a big commercial machine but the floor looked a lot better the next time I saw it.

At the dedication ceremony I learned I should have listened to Don Kinsman and stayed away. Most of the speakers reviewed how long it had taken and what a struggle it had been to raise enough money. They knew when to look my way and plant more seeds of resentment. One lady from the top of their command came to me and gave a long, drawn out sigh, "O-O-O-H. I'm glad that's over."

"That's all I can do." I told her. "I'm turning it over to you. The next thing I want is something to get the kids involved."

She was raising three daughters, nearly grown, and had often expressed her desire that the church should be a place for elegant weddings.

She let out another, "O-O-O-H" "Little kids make noises. And they spill things. Can't you keep them away 'till they grow up a little more??"

Before I got over the anger from that statement, her husband came to tell me, "Now you can get a real job and quit expecting the church to support you!"

The celebration was a big pot-luck dinner. One lady had donated the kitchen a nice shiny set of silverware. She worried herself into a frenzy; some piece might be lost or stolen. She pranced around looking over everyone's shoulder and wouldn't let anyone enjoy their meal as she counted the salad forks and soup spoons.

We attended church services there for a while. But we were never made to feel welcome. There was too much resentment and distrust. I'd helped build a place for them to get together and discuss ways to improve the morals of the people of the town. The men usually picked someone who appeared to have achieved financial success and spent the morning in a critical analysis of how he should spend his money. The women's conversation targeted any recently married woman and counted the days that passed between her wedding and the birth of her first child.

At the same time as I was working on the church building the preacher moved into the position of vice-chairman of the town council. He tried to joke about it, "Nothing to do, this town has no vice in it." He was in the middle of a war of personalities that caused me to have to look for jobs out of town. I'll describe those events in the next chapter.

My goal, getting my kids involved in church work, was fulfilled when a different church group built their own building. They studied the same Bible and welcomed me and my family—especially they welcomed my kids. There was just a different name on the sign over the front door and emphasis on a few different things in their methods of worship.

Neither the preacher nor any of the congregation asked us to come back after they knew we were gone. Some razzed us that we went to church only when we were being paid. We got one nice handwritten thank you note from Julius and Marie Williamson.

I don't need to identify which of the seven churches now in that town caused me all this misery. A few people are still here who know this story as well as I. A lot more don't care. I left with the hope those who are now attending can fulfill their spiritual needs in any kind of weather without concern about how that roof came to be built over their heads.

Chapter Three

RAN OUT OF TOWN (FOR PAYING MY BILLS)

One of my most traumatic experiences started with a package that arrived in the mail from the State Tax and Revenue Department. It accused me of tax evasion and threatened criminal prosecution while giving me my first notification I should have been paying gross receipts tax. They required me to trace my back trail for the previous three years, compute the tax; add penalties and interest and send it to them within seventy-two hours.

It was a pre-arranged scare scene. They forgave and forgot lots of people who they caught under similar circumstances. If a person had no money the state couldn't collect. I owned property they could attach so I had to comply.

Subsequent phone calls revealed they knew a lot about me. I'd been busting my butt to pay my bills at the local grocery store, thinking the man who owned it should appreciate my efforts. Local custom dictated that he give credit to everyone who shopped there and it was open knowledge his losses were staggering. A lot of our money came as small checks from neighbors which we used to pay for what we purchased in his store.

The town had recently become an incorporated village and this grocer was elected to be the first mayor. Now he was faced with the task of raising the revenue to operate this new government. He was quick to use his position of authority to carry out his personal vendettas. The town's principal source of funds came from part of the gross receipts tax. Five percent of everything sold there went to Santa Fe. One percent came back.

The search for money led the mayor and town council into taking a close look at everyone's business. Anyone who sold anything was a target. Peddlers selling apples or watermelons from the back of a truck parked on Main Street were a sitting duck for the mayor's wrath. There were also men who fed their families through the winter by selling firewood. One lady sold cosmetics. A man carried a catalog and took orders for mail order shoes. This scramble for cash required all of them to buy a five-dollar town business license and caused their names to be sent to the State Tax and Revenue Department to get them started paying the gross receipts tax. These money-hungry individuals involved with the town government followed the Construction Board guidelines and decided I should buy separate business licenses for carpentry, plumbing, painting and Thelma needed her own to reupholster old chairs.

I'd bought their license for carpentry even when I was giving away my time on the church. Thelma's upholstery business was outside the village limits but they ruled she needed the license to haul her work back to the owners. The grocer watched everyone from his store. One lady who was involved with the new town government worked in the post office. She knew no restraints on telling what she could learn about people's business from handling their mail.

Though I was working by the hour I ran afoul of a portion of the law that classified me as an independent contractor rather than a wage earner. If the people I worked for had been handling payroll withholding, Social Security and income tax, I would have been an employee, exempt from the sales tax. The rules were buried so deep in the fine print the town's own lawyer gave me wrong information. But a woman who asked me to crawl through the filthy mess when the sewer broke under her house trailer would not have had the books in place to handle payroll withholding. She barely had fifteen dollars in the bank to pay me for fixing the pipe. But this mayor watched our paper trail and reported it to Santa Fe. The service I'd performed came back to haunt me after we spent her money to buy groceries.

One of the thankless jobs I was handling for the community at the time was the maintenance of our community television translators. Satellite dishes hadn't yet been invented. People in cities got T.V. reception from rabbit ears or outdoor antennas. There were a few high peaks in our area where an antenna would pick up signals from the stations in Tucson, Arizona. Our primitive system on the top of those mountains was powered by four large automobile batteries. The signal was picked up on one antenna, run through the translator and rebroadcast to the town through another antenna. The viewer received it on another channel. Line of sight determined who watched T.V. Those who lived behind a hill might be out of luck. When everything worked we had three channels.

I kept a change of batteries on a charger at my home. When the ones at the translator got weak I loaded an old Jeep and made the trip to exchange them. It had to be done about every three weeks; oftener if windstorms messed up the alignment of the antennas or lightening storms blew fuses. If snow was on the ground it was necessary to crawl under the Jeep, with icy water dripping in my face, and put on four tire chains. No one cared how many other things I needed to do or how bad the weather might be. My phone rang if T. V. was bad when someone wanted to watch a ball game. They also called and cursed me when it was their antenna the wind had turned or if their lead-in wire broke and lay on the ground beside the pole.

A few volunteers assessed themselves five dollars a month, a fund that replaced batteries and equipment. They paid me ten-dollars a trip for use of my Jeep and Thelma frequently spent that to buy groceries.

When the lady from Tax and Revenue read me my list of illegal activities she mentioned that I was running a television repair business without paying any tax. The tax on ten-dollars would have been fifty cents, and the portion that came back to the town would have been a dime. It made me so mad I appeared at the front door of the store with the batteries and extra parts the next morning. When the mayor/grocer arrived to unlock, I told him, "If you want that dime so bad you can take the job that goes with it!"

I also told Thelma, "Pay our bill. Pay with a personal check and don't go back in that place!"

I recognized their need to raise revenue. But I'd been so concerned with just feeding my family I hadn't worried about the fine points of the law. I thought that if the few dollars they'd collect from me were so important, they should tell me about anything wrong with the way I was conducting my business before they carried my name and history to Santa Fe.

The mayor soon got his revenge.

I took a job building new restrooms on a bar, two doors away from his store.

Anyone connected with the town government could use the town telephone to talk to Santa Fe, even for personal vendettas.

Grouchy, the mayor hardly spoke, though he passed my job several times a day satisfying his craving for beer. I could see him through a door, seldom closed, that opened from my job onto the front sidewalk. He was watching my every move.

A stranger tapped my shoulder as I was rolling paint on the walls. He stuck a badge in my face and announced, "I'm Cliff Cochran, State Plumbing Inspector. I want to see your license! I want to see your permit! And I want to see what kind of pipe you used down there!" He pointed at our new concrete floor.

The mayor picked that moment to poke his head through that open door and laugh.

The building inspector played his cards to get as much mileage as he could out of a scare scene. I'd bought the plumbing tree from a contractor who made sure I was putting together a legal design. He'd numbered the fittings with a felt pen to help me assemble the drain in the right order. The inspector's comment was, "It's a beautiful job, but I'm going to hang you for doing it without a license!"

Sid Jones, owner of the bar thwarted the inspector's command that I break the concrete. Recent throat surgery had left him unable to speak. He'd always had a problem with stuttering and now was writing notes to communicate with me. His message to the inspector was clear, "L-L-L-Like H-H-Hell Y-Y-You're G-G-Goin' a B-B-Break any C-Concrete. It's M-M-Mine. I've P-P-Paid for it!"

The result got me more familiar with the State Construction Commission. It had been foisted on the public under the guise of consumer protection. The result put more people on a state payroll, collected more taxes and impeded the progress of the jobs they regulated.

I had partially completed a home that I was building for resale and thus far I'd been working on a home owner's permit. The inspector refused to allow me to go ahead until I got my own plumber's license. He promised to be helpful if I'd cooperate, saying, "We need to get someone that is qualified in this area." I learned those contractor's licenses come at considerably more effort and expense than walking to a sporting goods counter and buying a fishing license. The finishing work on my home was delayed for years until I studied books, passed tests and met the state requirements for financial responsibility.

When the inspector and I were able to meet on friendlier terms he readily admitted our first encounter was a result of a complaint that had come from the town mayor.

I wasn't through stacking the deck against myself in my dealings with the town government.

One lady was bouncing between jobs in the post office and as secretary for the town government. She raised two sons with very little discipline or moral guidance. One of them discovered some unusual fruit trees on my land a short distance from my home. The apples are unique, almost as large as a cantaloupe. This kid was making regular trips driving by my house without stopping or giving any explanation. Then someone told me he was selling these large apples in town.

On his next trip I caught him with a ten-pound potato sack full of apples on the pickup seat. I scolded him, "If you had the decency to stop and ask, I'd give them to you! I don't have time to pick them! But if you're going to steal them and sell them you are going to have to give me half of what you're making!"

That lady thought her kids did no harm. My stopping the boy triggered a tantrum and hatred that lasted for years. No more than an hour passed and she was at my front gate, her pickup bumper nearly dragging the ground with a heavy load of apples. She'd injured a foot or ankle. Though wrapped in a bandage it didn't keep her from climbing to the top of the load wearing a neat pink pantsuit. She grabbed an apple, threw it at my house and informed me, "Your brains are made of shit!" When she hurled the next apple she screamed, "Thelma's brains are made of shit!" She had some similar description of one or both of us to go with each apple on that load. She bellowed and howled threats about how we were going to be prosecuted for everything we were doing without a license, especially Thelma's little business in the middle of our living room, reupholstering old furniture.

She drove away when her pickup was empty and our roof, yard, and the front wall of our house were well decorated with pulp of smashed apples.

However she didn't waste all her apples. In our mailbox we'd find discarded cores, pop bottles and other lunch scraps.

This lady had her hand in supplying the information that was being fed to the mayor and the town council. Now she could bombard me with building inspectors and tax collectors and she often bragged that anyone who ever made her mad would never be allowed to forget it.

I'd put the church building together for a preacher who was now vice-chairman of the town council but who denied knowing about the troubles they had brought me through the Tax and Revenue Department, the Construction Commission, or the mad lady in the post office. It was easy for me to assume he treated his responsibilities to the town with the same detached indifference as he had the construction of the church. He may not have known what was happening. Yet I always knew churches were supposed to bring a turning point in people's lives. My turning point came when they all got together to run me out of town.

One building inspector, Bill Cooper, had always had a friendly attitude. But a day came that he made a noisy scene of squealing brakes, sliding tires and flying dust and gravel when he stopped is car in front of my job. "I've got a report on you!" He was feigning anger uncommon to his nature. "You've been seen with a paint brush!"

"No, I bid on a paint job. But I didn't get it. Someone else wanted it cheaper." I answered. Obviously he had heard something about a request from the County Commission to repaint the inside of the court house.

"You can't do that! It's not in the scope of the license you got for plumbing!"

"The guy that got it isn't licensed for anything." I answered.

"He has nothing to loose." Cooper showed a hint of a smile.

"What difference does it make? Is the State just trying to get in my pocket for another $100.00 bill?"

"That's part of it. But the main thing is you've made people mad. They have a copy of the list of license categories." He pointed to the new home I was building. "I saw you leveling the ground, pouring concrete. You've done framing and roofing and painting—the only license you have is for plumbing. There are probably at least twenty-five specialty stages. Or if you had a General Contractors License you could hire licensed subcontractors for each of these steps. It's not feasible for you or me! But these people hate you! They call Santa Fe and Santa Fe calls me! I've got all I can handle with the new work that's happening around Tyrone and Plyas, but when my boss calls me I have to drive all the way up here to chew your rear!''

"Are those reports coming out of City Hall?" I asked. "They have a mad secretary sitting in the driver's seat. The mayor and council let her run the whole show. None of them will stand up to her."

The inspector nodded affirmative. "It'll save you and me both a bunch of headaches if you'll get out of the damned town! Find work that's outside their jurisdiction. Do you know where the town limits are?"

I answered, "Yes, and I'll buy your lunch for that information."

''Thanks, but I was sent up here to shut you down. We'd best not be seen together." Every job I took for the next four years was outside of Reserve. There were cabins at Willow Creek, Quemado Lake and on the East side of the county near Beaverhead. There was a fire-damage job on a lady's roof in Blue River. Some of the jobs came in Nutrioso and Eager, Arizona. I worried that I'd soon be in trouble for making a living in two states.

One of the best places to work was on the Farr Ranch, well hidden from building inspectors and tax collectors, near Horse Springs. Out there on the Augustine Plains the wind blew cold.

Dave Farr said it is, "Just a breeze until it starts throwing rocks at you."

The Farr's promised to use their guns if any inspector appeared on the place. When they wrote a check it was good—and their building code was simple—no pay until they were satisfied with the work.

We attended church most Sundays, after the sermon the preacher always walked to the door and shook everyone's hand as they left. He never failed to ask me where I was working or what I was doing. I saw no reason not to tell him.

After the grocer who had been the mayor died of cancer and the preacher moved up to that position I received a mimeographed form letter from the Village, bearing the preacher's signature, bluntly reminding me I hadn't renewed my town license and threatening that they'd cause the State Tax and Revenue Department to audit my books if I neglected it. This sounded like the secretary—I'd regularly told the preacher where I was working.

I mailed their letter back but along the bottom I wrote, "Shove your town tax up you're a_ _. The town of Reserve knows to find me when they want a church building donated, but paying jobs are fifty-miles away." This should have changed his act if he was letting the secretary run the town business.

Their response was another mimeographed form letter. This one threatened to place liens on property for unpaid taxes. That too was signed by this preacher who was also the mayor.

This time I reacted by changing churches. My written response was, "I don't trust a man to guide me to the Promised Land if he can't find the Village limits of the town where he is Mayor."

I had to fight one more battle with the town council before they quit keeping such a close watch on my business. Another change of mayors brought a high-school janitor, Earnestina Zuniga, to hold the top office. The same mean tempered secretary continued to run the town.

I'd made another enemy when I got a plumber's license. This man owned the town water system, sold propane and was licensed as an electrician. He considered whatever licenses he held as a membership in a private club that was supposed to keep all competitors out of the way. People who needed help fixing their pipes were supposed to wait until he got ready and pay his price.

Information had been passed to me from the plumbing inspector that indicated he wasn't licensed for half the jobs he took. But he was very unhappy when he heard I got a license. He went to the town council for their help when he had an axe to grind.

I was in the middle of a gamble that I hoped would bring my work closer to home and yield greater profits. Some of the houses I'd built were sold before they were completed. The people who hired me then made a healthy profit. Tired of driving 100-miles everyday with gasoline prices going up, it appeared to be a wise decision to use a vacant lot I owned inside the town limits and build a home for resale. I used a home-owner's permit as if that is where I was going to live. I further reasoned that until it sold I hadn't made any money so I didn't need the town's business license.

The day I broke ground, that job became a thorn in the secretary's side. She sent me an application for an excavator's license. I threw it in the trash. When we were working on the foundation she sent one for masonry. True to   Inspector Cooper's warning, she followed the list of categories of specialty licenses that were available from the Construction Commission. She must have hoped I'd send her five-dollars for each thing I did. I discarded her applications weekly as the job progressed through framing, roofing, painting and landscaping.

That house stood partially completed for several years as I scraped together time and money to proceed. All this time the town council was watching for some chance to catch me in a trap. This unhappy plumber played into their hands when he went to them with a complaint that, "Charlie hooked to your sewer without a permit. I saw him do it."

They took his word as he had to drive by my job to get to his home.

They sent me a letter, signed by this new mayor, telling me I was in violation of a town ordinance and that I'd have to dig up the connection and get it inspected by the man who ran their wastewater plant.

I'd never connected that sewer. The house was vacant and I didn't want to make unnecessary monthly water and sewer payments. This work was to be left undone until I found a buyer.

I mailed them an answer knowing other people in the town were unhappy with interference that was coming into their lives from the City Hall. "That house drain ends in an open ditch in the front yard, easily inspected by anyone who is interested." I nailed copies of their letter and mine to a bulletin board on Main Street in the middle of town.

The town gossips got their amusement for the week and a few newspaper articles were written about the incident. My retort may have influenced a turning point in their attitude because it was the last trouble to come to me from City Hall. After a few more years the secretary became friendly and had me deliver material orders to her yard.

Cochran, the state plumbing inspector, had demanded I get that plumbing license, claiming it would be good for my business and necessary for the town. But his actions the first time I called for an inspection reinforced my dislike for anyone who used their government job as a reason to meddle with my business. I'd built two cabins for a father and son near Quemado Lake. They wanted ground disturbance to be held to a minimum and asked me to combine the plumbing drains so both cabins emptied into the same septic system. I consulted Cochran to find out if there were any problems or restrictions. His answer was, "You'd better put in a fifteen-hundred gallon septic tank."

I was laughed at all over Albuquerque when I tried to buy that size. "What are you building, a hotel?" One plumbing contractor learned the name of my inspector and said, "He used to be here—gave us so many problems we got him ran out of town." He sold me a one-thousand gallon tank, gave me his business card, and said, "If he doesn't approve it, you call me. I'll come out there and help you shove him in it!"

I was nervous, everything in the ground but nothing covered. The tank filled with water and backfill against the sides but exposed on top. How would I salvage my investment if he failed to approve? Cochran got to the job wearing a heavy smell of alcohol. He kept a hand on his car as he walked around it, carefully hanging onto something to maintain his balance. He spent several moments looking up the hill toward the cabins then back to the tank and leach field. He growled, "You know damn well you can't get water to flow from here up there." I was dealing with a State Inspector who couldn't figure out which direction the waste water flowed.

The next time I called for an inspection it was on the new home I built for resale, the one Cochran refused to permit until I got a license. I told my buyer, who was an insurance adjuster that the final inspection had never been done for the plumbing.

"Is Cliff Cochran your inspector?

"Yes."

"Don't worry. The plumbing passed." He assured me. Then he smiled and explained, "There was a D.W.I. incident that totaled a state car. I had to get him out of trouble! Don't worry. That plumbing passed."

Chapter Four

1981 NECESSITY AND INSPIRATION

The more I had become involved with home building the more necessary it became to construct my own shop building and a place to store some of the basic building materials.

For tool storage I was using a little log cabin that had been Dad's blacksmith shop. I'd accumulated enough tools, when I unloaded them there I had to climb over the boxes to close the door. My arc welder was in an old beverage machine to keep it out of the weather and I found myself doing cabinet jobs behind a tarp in a sandstorm. Maintenance work like grease jobs and oil changes were usually postponed for a stormy day making it necessary to wallow in a mud puddle. The building material that I tried to keep on hand was in haphazard piles in an old hay barn. Handling was wearing out gypsum wallboard before it could be used and the mixed grades of plywood meant the piece that was needed was always on the bottom.

I drew several sketches of different barn arrangements. Wanting enough height to cover a truckload of hay, space to use a table saw while more than one project went unfinished, tool storage, and bins to sort different thicknesses of plywood, everything I designed turned into a monster. Thelma was reupholstering furniture in the middle of our living room. Larger items like couches and recliners would be torn apart for weeks. On Friday evenings the local logging company, owned by Lem Fryar, sent   her a pile of diesel-stained foam cushions or dirty truck seats and a request that she have them ready to take to the job at 4:00 a.m. Monday. She needed her own space.

We followed a family habit of making do with what we had. The only equipment I could put on the job was an old flatbed truck, a farm tractor with a front loader, and a chain saw. I'd spent years collecting a large pile of used metal roofing. It was random lengths and beat up but the heavy rust only penetrated one side. Seven miles away there was a juniper thicket that would make good tall posts. Used cinder block came from a clean-up job.

We picked a spot of soft dirt and started to construct a 56x56 ft. barn. To get the ground level I had to dig five feet deep at the back to get the front doors arranged to get equipment inside the front. People from town asked if we were building an airplane hanger.

From a few small jobs, sale of some cull cows, and collection of some money people owed us we scrounged the cash to buy a new metal roof and some framing lumber. Four rows of tall posts soon stood with beams on top. The two middle rows were tallest with everything calculated to get the necessary roof slope.

That home I'd built for resale had become my albatross. I'd started it on a bank loan at ten and a half percent interest. The banker renewed the loan several times at rising rates before I got it sold. He was now getting seventeen percent. No real estate was selling. Then I got a buyer and got rid of it. I was free of debt and didn't know how to act. I knew for sure I wasn't going to let myself get into that kind of a mess again. Enough money came from the deal to pay off the banker. The rest was going to come in monthly payments of $382.00 a month—the first time in my life I could look ahead and see promise of steady money coming. I was determined to put it into more business growth. The people in town blabbed about how I ran my business and they thought I was wealthy. The asking price of the home had been common knowledge. Stories that came to me indicated they assumed it had cost nothing to build. They didn't know about any discounts I'd had to give to get it to move, and I must have got the whole amount before the new owners moved in. Then their yarns grew bigger as word spread around town that I was going to stock some lumber. Anything they might ever need was going to be there when they needed it.

My plans of keeping a few pieces of lumber and plywood grew on people's wish lists to be a full fledged lumber yard. They wanted a home center, then a complete shopping mall. Each built his own plans around what he'd expect us to sell. They came to us wanting to know how soon we'd have pet supplies, garden seeds and sporting goods. I had to explain to each I was planning a little backyard business where they could find some of the basics. No one gave any thought to how I'd pay for any of it. One day Lem Fryar came on the scene. No equipment seats for Thelma that day, he was carrying a cold six-pack of beer which he sat on top of a saw horse. "Hear ya goin' a sell building material." He popped open a can for each of us.

Lem's steady business had been good for Thelma's upholstery shop but he'd fired me twice from building jobs. I didn't count him on my list of best friends.

I explained, "There are a lot of stories going around, but I'm not planning enough to even call it a store. This is a shop—a place out of the weather to keep my tools. I'll keep a few sacks of cement, and what I can afford of the things that go into every job."

"I think you got the right idea." Lem opened two more beers. I hadn't finished my first. "I'll buy all I can from you."

I thought the beer was talking—he was wasting my time. I remembered the first time he fired me. He'd hired me to add some rooms to his home, pointed out a refrigerator in his shop that was always filled with beer and told me, "Help yourself."

It was hard for me to know when he was serious. He liked to joke but he wanted everything done right. All the building lines had to run straight. He'd made me tear up a few things and do them over because he wasn't going to accept any sloppy work. He could be totally displeased yet smile like he was trying to be funny.

That day he'd spent a bunch of time harping that the job was going too slow. Then he was gone for a while and came back complaining I'd put in a window crooked.

"Did you get into my beer while I was gone?" He asked.

We double-checked with two levels.

At the most it may have needed a quarter-inch correction in the length of an eight foot window. But along the bottom there was a similar mistake in the opposite direction on a horizontal strip of siding. Close examination revealed a half inch triangle that would have been covered when we put on the trim. He wasn't going to accept it or pay for the time to correct it. He got another carpenter to finish the job.

We drank beer while I explained that the shop wasn't going to be half large enough to store what people wanted. I didn't have any money to buy inventory--didn't know where to get it—and knew absolutely nothing about running a retail business.

Lem opened the last two beers. "You've got to start somewhere. I started with one old truck." That was true. He'd come to town working as a mechanic. Then he dug around several scrap piles and assembled what would be the most hopeless looking piece of junk into a truck that hauled logs with the best of the whole string of worn-out rigs. He kept it working and gave it a coat of paint. Now he owned the best looking truck. When other drivers went home in the evening he gave his a wash job. He kept resurrecting abandoned machinery until he owned several bulldozers, log skidders, loaders and a whole fleet of trucks.

His business grew from that one truck to the point where he employed several dozen men. Any broken machine stopped their production. His crew supplied the sawmill which fed the businesses around town. Like a row of dominoes, everything could collapse if the logs stopped coming off that mountain.

When a machine broke he worked all night to put it back in service. He was making several trips to Albuquerque each week to purchase the tires and parts.

Lem finished three beers before I got through my first but he'd opened all six. "You've got to drink them," I told him. "Two's my limit." I tried to tell him how important it was becoming for me to have on hand some of the things I needed. Customers changed their plans. Mistakes were made that wasted material. Small jobs came up. If I couldn't put my hands on a few essential items I'd have to run to town every day.

"I know it—better than you." My cans of unfinished beer were waiting in a row and he'd gone back to his pickup for another six-pack. "I've worn out five pickups on that road to Albuquerque. Now, if I have to go to buy brake shoes for a truck, I buy for two. That'll save me a trip some day."

I had to insist he not open any more beer for me. I was thinking about the second time he'd fired me. He'd searched all over town to find me then said, I've got to have a plumber—fast."

"I'll be here a few more days." I told him. "I like to finish one job before I go to another."

"Not this time! He told me. He went on to explain that he'd bought a big new metal building for a shop. "It will be here next week. The people I bought it from are going to put it together. But I have to have the floor ready.

"I want some bathrooms in it!" He urged. "You better get down there fast! I ordered the concrete this morning! The trucks will be here in about two hours!"

"I can't do it!" I told him. "I'd have to get the permit! I'd have to go somewhere and get the material! I need to know what fixtures go in it. How many bathrooms? Will they have hot water? You should have come to me last week!"

Lem wasn't going to take "No" for an answer. "We couldn't have used you last week. We had to bring a 'Cat' down here and get the ground ready. Garfield thinks he has enough material. I tried to get him to do it but he doesn't have the time and I don't give a damn about any permit!"

"If I do it, I'll have to do it by code!" I told him firmly. "I put a lot of work into getting a plumbing license and they tell me how to do the job. I'll have to send in the permit. The pipes will have to be inspected before you can pour concrete over them."

"Fine—if you can do it before the cement trucks get here! Garfield says you can go over to his place and pick up what you need. Just keep a list!"

At Merle Garfield's place I loaded what might be needed to put together the under the floor parts of two bathrooms. Fryar had given me no plan, but he'd said bathrooms—and that indicated more than one. Garfield was the one who wanted exclusive rights to do all the plumbing in the town. He's the one who had gone to the town council complaining about a sewer pipe I'd never installed.

Was this job a peace offering or was he leading me into a trap? This shop was a commercial job and my license was residential. The most plausible explanation was that by selling the material he had a chance to get a dollar he wouldn't get otherwise. Why didn't I just have the guts to say "No- Hell no?"

Whatever inner command that always drove me to help people when they needed it is what pushed me to take that job. Fryar gave me two men with picks and shovels to do the digging. There was no way the mechanics would keep a bathroom clean enough for a woman. The lady who handled his bookkeeping should have her own facilities near an upstairs office. This made it a stacked plumbing tree for vent purposes. Garfield's stock of parts didn't have what the code required. My neck would be on the chopping block at inspection time. "Somewhere over there in that corner, we'll make it fit was all he could give me for a plan."

Working in a rush, all I could do was lay a drain pipe across the ditch for the foundation and turn it up for the toilets. To try to pacify an inspector I planned two restrooms on separate drains that would come together outside the house.

The concrete crew was almost ready to cover me up when I stubbed in some branches for sinks and vents, blocked out a part of the floor so we could come back with a supply line and got out of their way.

I sure didn't need any more fights with a plumbing inspector. So I was running several alibis through my mind about why I didn't keep all my ducks in a proper row with the construction rules. I knew I should have waited for an inspection before this work was covered.

The next day while Fryar was admiring his new concrete floor he called me to the job. "Thanks for getting down here and helping us out. But I'd like to know what you're going to do with all those pipes sticking up."

He was in that mood that I didn't know if he was mad or trying to joke with me. Previous experience told me to proceed with caution. When he pointed out a 2 inch pipe beside a 3 inch pipe I explained that the small one was a vent, required by code, that would go up to the second floor.

I tried to tell him that as water went down a pipe it pushed air ahead. Replacement air had to come through that vent to make the system drain better. "We don't need that!" Now there was no doubt that he was unhappy. "There ain't goin'a be any damn inspector tell me how to build my stuff!" He fired me again.

Now I was drinking beer with a man who had fired me twice. I'd come to admire him for what he could accomplish with worn-out machinery. I appreciated the steady business he was giving Thelma in her upholstery shop, but I didn't place much value on anything he told me. That dismissal gave me an easy way to avoid collisions with an inspector. I'd just forget to send in a permit.

I judged him wrong! I was underestimating the value of a steady customer.

Lem's life changed. He suffered hard luck or tragedy on every turn but he kept coming back to place orders at my store. More than once he was injured in accidents. Workers wrecked several of the trucks. He came home one day to find his wife dead without advance warning or plausible explanation. Then a log dropped off a truck and crushed one of his sons below the waist. The young man had to spend the rest of his life with paralyzed legs. Politics entered the picture and protection of the spotted owl stopped the harvesting of logs to make lumber. Now he didn't need his new shop or the machinery he had spent years accumulating.

When he had to remodel his home to accommodate a wheelchair for the handicapped boy he sent the workers to me for supplies. He never stopped. Some project that involved building or remodeling was in progress all the time. When age and health problems stopped him from doing anything else he capped all that with an order for a chain link fence around his property. He might haggle and look for the best deal before he started a job but his payment always came-in full and on time--sometimes without waiting to be billed at the end of the month.

As I look back counting my good and bad experiences I have to say I got more encouragement from a beer-charged logger than any other person in my trade area.

Firmly believing the best place to look for advice is from someone who has 'been there and done that,' I appreciated every moment I could spend with Coleman Duncum. He and his wife, Bertha, came to Reserve, some fifteen summers to escape the heat of Cameron, Texas. He'd been a farmer and in retail business all his life. When our business was in its infancy he enjoyed helping around the store. He was deeply religious, with a personality that could put a smile on the face of the maddest customer. They had no doubt he'd reached his limit when they were trying to get a lower price.

I needed help when I was figuring how to add in all the hidden costs of running a business. The people on the street who accused me of robbing them obviously didn't think they should be paying toward the insurance, taxes, power and telephone or even the payroll costs. The cash register count at the end of day had to yield enough to cover all that overhead and put the merchandise back on the shelf before we could say we'd made a dime. How was I to figure that part when I wrote the price tag?

Coleman gave me a little horse sense that saved a lot of complicated book-keeping. He said, "Add it up at the end of the month and figure it as a percent of your monthly turnover; do that a few months and you'll get a pretty good average." Then he went on, "Quit trying to just break even. If you haven't made anything—you've lost money. If you lose for many months you won't stay here."

Coleman put his church work first, but he wanted to help me and he was looking for tax deductions. This church was new to me. I'd changed to it after many stupid arguments with the congregation where I'd assembled a new building. We needed a kitchen and a room to meet for pot-luck dinners. He told me, "Figure up what you need for the material." He had his checkbook in his hand as he said it.

"I can't answer that for a few days," I told him. "I'll have to draw a plan—count the boards—there'll be windows and shingles and things I don't have. I'll have to call and get the cost."

"I didn't say cost!" He interrupted. "I want you to make some money!"

This was a shocking change. I thought all customers wanted everything as cheap as they could get it. I thought all churches were struggling and begging for donations for everything they received. Though Coleman repeatedly told me he wanted me to make some money I couldn't bring myself to accept any monetary profit from anything I did for a church. He even offered to pay for my labor as I pre-cut and led the assembly of the job.

This addition was behind the main building. People who drove the road out front could only get a quick glimpse of new lumber as they passed. I ran that job with no permits or inspections and found myself surprised when we got it done with no interruption from anyone else in the town.

A few years later our preacher, his wife and four children were crammed into a single wide house trailer the church furnished for their home. Coleman again had his checkbook in his hand when he told me to figure out what it would cost to add two rooms. This time he repeated that he wanted me to make some money. I was just as stubborn when I told him that whether I "Sink or Swim, it won't be on the dollars I take from a church."

Coleman was a small man but I looked up to him. We had lots of other people who made their money somewhere else then came to our mountains to spend it. These were the people who supported my builder's supply business in a community that was being killed by the politics of the time. Most of them built a mansion then put it behind a locked gate and a "No Trespassing" sign. Coleman put his tax deduction to work where it was a benefit to the people who stayed.

I didn't plunge into the retail business. It was a slow stumbling process—like a baby's first steps—looking for some way to pull myself back up each time I fell. Now as I look back on those events that happened thirty years ago I see I received inspiration as a kid from a successful preacher. It was revived from a church leader but I may have never made a move without the encouragement of a frustrated logger who raised his spirits with drinks that contained alcohol.

I'd just passed age forty when I started stocking merchandise with the plan of selling it. My plan was to keep only the things I used on my jobs and to purchase manageable quantities so there would be no cause for alarm if no customers came. It would be only a little backyard business for the convenience of my neighbors and me. I was young, inexperienced and optimistic and had no clue of the problems, actions and attitudes that were waiting in ambush when I went around the next corner.

If my eyes had been fully open I'd have noticed that I'd never heard anything but blasphemy about any other local merchant. All of them had left a legacy as greedy individuals who stocked too little and charged much.

Those attitudes even came through our own family. I had one uncle in town, who I respected, and another uncle selling tires in Silver City who had gone broke in a store in our town during the Depression. He gave too many families their groceries on credit. The local uncle would break into very irreverent language when he talked about the other. He thought those bad debts were a deserved and justified reward for not marking cheaper prices.

The uncle in Silver City never rested until he'd paid off every cent of the debts he'd built up while trying to help the people in Reserve. There were very few still around who knew him when I ran my store and they considered all merchants to be crooks.

I was ignorant, naïve and gullible. Somehow I thought things would go better for me.

Chapter Five

IF YOUR TOWN GETS BEHIND YOU

The flow of events in the 1970's pushed me to where it was inevitable that I'd get into some degree of retail business selling building material. I needed to build a dry place to store supplies at the start of a job and needed room to come back with the leftovers at the finish. There was no place in the county to find those things so my neighbors beat a path to my door to see if I'd help them.

With no bookkeeping system to know my cost, it usually meant digging through a pile of old receipts to get an out-dated price. One neighbor, who always tried to get as much as possible without paying anything, devised a way to short-cut that problem. If it was something he could find on an advertised special in junk mail he'd bring the ad along to tell me, "Here's what it's selling for."

Some items, like 2x4 studs, came at a cheaper price and there was less spoilage if I bought a full bundle. Any leftover from one job would always carry forward to the next and I knew what was on the top of the pile. If I could use junk to make temporary blocking or braces I cleaned up waste that couldn't be put into the rest of the job.

Another thorn in my side was having half the town mad at me—watching for a chance to make a derogatory remark—after all the squabbling that came from the church and the town council. I deluded myself into thinking that if I provided a service they needed.—If I could save them a trip out of town—they might show some appreciation. I might regain a few friends.

To get advice and to get started with some of the first items I'd buy to keep on hand I went to the lumber yard where I'd been getting most of what went into my construction projects. That was Eddie Peter, at Ranchero Building Supply in Belen, NM.

Eddie led me into his office and closed the door. "What is on your mind?" He asked.

I kidded him. "You're sure getting gray fast." I'd been buying from him for twenty years,--didn't like his personality but trusted his advice. In that time his hair had changed from shiny black to snow white.

"Your sign says wholesale retail. I'm thinking about starting a little backyard business and getting you to be my supplier."

"Do you have any idea what problems you're asking for? You'll turn gray too."

"No. But I know we need some of this stuff a whole lot closer. I've been buying back the scraps and leftovers at the end of each job because they usually come in handy somewhere else. The whole town knows I've got them." I went on, "I can't eat supper when I get home in the evening. Someone will be there to buy a two by four or a scrap of plywood for their little job."

"Is this going to be a hobby or a business?"

"I'll have to make it pay its own way. That is why I wanted to ask you about wholesale pricing if I am buying it for resale."

"How much do you plan to buy at a time?" He was setting his sights on a bigger order than I could afford.

"I'd like to start with a few boards of each size and each length."

"Can you use a bundle of each size?"

"Not for a start. I was thinking more like a dozen of each length 2x4's from eight feet to sixteen long."

"That is retail!" He raised his voice wanting me to give him a serious order or get out. "We are giving you the best prices we can on that size order when we give you a contractor discount. When we put a man out there counting boards one at a time it costs us money. You can't get a wholesale price anywhere unless you take full packages with no hand handling!"

"You are shooting away out beyond what I can afford." I could see I might get in debt over my head real fast.

"You're going to start a business! Just how much money can you put your hands on?" He moved between me and the door.

"I think I can get my banker to let me have $10,000.00."

I'd come to him hoping he might be receptive to starting a branch store or a partnership. Maybe he'd consent to owning the stock and let me sell it. If he read my thoughts he squelched them fast. Eddie went into a violent laughing fit. I wanted to walk out but he blocked my way. He became so hysterical he started choking. I was humiliated and embarrassed. There was nothing I could do but wait until he regained his composure.

"I don't want to discourage you, but you can't start a business on $10,000.00! You won't have enough on hand to get people in your door."

"They are coming now. Sometimes a four foot scrap is all they need. It saves them a trip to town."

Eddie turned sarcastic. "That's a flea market! Old Charlie, the Good Samaritan drove his truck almost 400 miles to get a board to sell. Did you get him to pay you $500 to make it worth your while?"

"I was hoping I could get you to tell me what percent of mark up I could hope for if I get into this. If I'm too high they will come up here and get it themselves.''

"That's what we're here for." Eddie became more calm and collected. "Mark-up is up to you. But you'll have to recover all your costs. When you turn the key in that truck in the morning you know you have to fill the fuel tank but that isn't half the cost of running it."

"I know."

He went on. "You have to buy tires, and oil and insurance. When you get the load home you have the cost of your storage space and more insurance." He hesitated. "Do you have a forklift?"

"That will come later, if we move enough material to justify it."

"Oh, my aching back!" His convulsions of laughter started again. "You've got the nerve! I think you'll die of old age before you get this business going!"

"Well I'm going to try it. I don't want to buy a thing I can't pull out of stock and use on my own jobs. It will sure be handy to have around."

"How many people live out there?" He asked.

"I think it is about a thousand."

"That's not many. You know we have around one hundred thousand within five miles north and south." He paused. "You'll have to remember each one of them is important. And even though you might not like some of them, their money is all the same color of green. When you clean out the cash drawer at night you can't tell which dollar came from your best friend."

We concluded the visit with Eddie telling me, "If your town gets behind you, it might work. You're providing a service they should appreciate. And they should be willing to pay for it."

"They're behind me now." It was my turn to try for humor. "That's one of the reasons I'm doing this. I got ran out of town about five years ago. I paid my grocery bill, and built a church, and stopped a kid from stealing apples. Those three things offended enough people that they ran me out of town. I'm trying to help them but honestly I never saw them do anything but bitch about anyone else that had a store there. Since then I've drove 100 miles a day for every nail I pounded. This venture, if it works, will bring me back home. We are nearly a mile outside the Village limits so there won't be any town licenses or tax."

I'd talked when I should have been listening. It took twenty years to realize how much wisdom, experience, and warning Eddie wrapped into a few words when he said, "If your town gets behind you."

If I had to buy full bundles I'd be looking at more than a semi-truck load of weight in the first order—not practical to plan to bring it home on my eighteen-year old ton-and-a half truck. It would entail a lot more investment than I planned. Our little business was going to have to turn enough dollars to justify what we were putting into it. I was exploring new territory. The only way to get some idea of what lay ahead was to ask someone who had already been down that road. And there were a lot of people who hadn't been there, who were only interested in satisfying their own needs, anxious to point me in the wrong direction if they found a chance. I entered the business with the same philosophy a rancher uses when he buys a cow. He has to hand over his money and hope for the best because there is no way to know if she will raise a calf.

Chapter Six

SUPPLIERS NEEDED

We only had a small stack of leftovers when word got around that we were going to sell building material. Within days that story had expanded to where we would put in a full service lumber yard, a home center that stocked hardware, appliances and garden supplies.

We saw it as a challenge, an opportunity to build a business from scratch. It would take time to put together enough merchandise to call it a store. We knew we'd make mistakes but our optimism kept us from knowing how serious they would be.

The demand came as if we only had to rub a magic lamp and anything someone wanted would come floating down out of the sky. Customers were impatient, anything they wanted should be here now, but we had to move forward one step at a time. We hoped we could make a dollar and reinvest it so the business should help itself grow.

Our clients wouldn't tolerate our plan to work with a few dollars at a time and customers asked, "Do you have it?" or "Can you get it?" Even if we had no idea where to find it, they'd ask, "How much is it?" Many more of them were arrogant and followed with "Why don't you?" Many queries for things we didn't have progressed to a foot stomping, door slamming third stage that ended with "Oh Shit! They make it! You should have it." None saw any connection between the speed of turnover and what we could afford to stock.

There was a small hardware store in town and the last thing I wanted to do was compete with them. I thought it would help their business if I sold things they didn't stock. My reasoning was, "If people didn't have to go out of town to get lumber, cement, and plywood, then they might also buy their paint and screws locally."

Many buildings in town had been built of rough-green lumber, direct from the sawmill. Boards that were fit tight together in a wall or floor shrank as they dried and left inch wide cracks. The bandsaw that was cutting it wobbled to leave uneven thickness that might vary from a half-inch at one end to two inches at the other, A customer had to work with whatever length came down the chain. I was tired of the hassle.

Surfaced lumber was my first priority so I went to Stone Forest Industries, the company that was running the local sawmill. They cut rough green lumber before it was trucked to a planer mill and dry kiln sixty-five miles away at Eagar, Arizona. Then the finished product moved to wholesalers nationwide. This was happening at a time when interest rates had peaked, the housing market was at a standstill and the mill had laid off their night shift to run at half capacity. They didn't sell to contractors. But I'd used lots of their lumber. They sent orders to their employees and had made a special promotional deal for the church job. Whatever history they had about me came from contacts I'd made when I worked on their company houses, jobs I'd done for their workers, and most recently on the church job.

Salesman, Skip Shrigley, tried to stop me before I got started in my first buying call. "We don't sell to contractors."

"No, I want to open a small retail lumber business."

"How many feet are you going to buy?" I could sense his lack of interest.

"A package each of 2x4's and 2x6's eight to sixteen feet."

"I'll call you back. I'll call you right back." Shrigley hung up the phone without asking for my number. He snubbed a chance to sell thirty three thousand board feet of lumber because his company didn't want to be bothered with small orders.

I made a contact with Joe Rosser who ran his own truck to supply a lumber yard in El Paso, Texas. There were no truck scales between Eagar and my store so he was willing to carry a package or two more than a legal load then take the time to help me pull it off by hand at my place.

Rosser cautioned me, "I opened my store with a $100,000.00 loan and made a bet the first five people would ask for something I didn't have. He paused. "Three of them did."

Rosser got us started. If his truck was empty when he left El Paso he brought us small orders of plywood or roofing.

Reserve, New Mexico now had a pile of the most basic building material. But I'd spent the $10,000.00 I'd borrowed to get started. The interest bill was ticking and the top of the lumber pile would spoil if it didn't sell. It was time to let our neighbors know it was here and they didn't have to go out of town.

My hopes soared when the first builder came to look at our stock. My selection of 2x4's and 2x6's would cover the needs of ninety percent of the things I'd built. His project was a small porch and I didn't have a 2x12 to make the step. He left saying, "Oh, hell if I have to go out of town for that board I might as well get it all."

The next potential customer needed nails and paint. I said, "We aren't into hardware. You can get that at the store in town."

"What kind of a building supply is this? No nails and no paint!" We had disappointed him too.

Then a man sneered, "I hear you ain't got nothin' but wood."

"We're starting out with the basic lumber." I tried to be polite.

"That's all I need. Gimme a new axe handle."

A good friend asked for, "Four good ten-foot 2x4's."

"There they are. You're the first one to get into the pile."

He tossed the top layer out of his way. Then he picked up each board and eyed it like sighting a rifle, discarding anything with a slight crown. He checked the knots, looked at small drying cracks and refused anything with a little bark on a corner. When he was halfway through the bundle, a half-hour job was waiting for me to re-stack it, and he'd selected two boards.

"I'm sorry," I interrupted him. "I can't sell lumber that way."

"What's wrong?"

"I gave the same price for those boards you are discarding as I did for the ones you are keeping! And I'm not making enough to throw many away. I want the next person that gets in that pile to have the same chance as you to get the best lumber!"

"Then I don't need them!" He left the pile in disarray and walked out the door.

I was doing worse that Rosser. Four customers had come in and out—no sale—and all of them left unhappy.

A request came for me to do a roofing job. I could use my lumber but it would take about half bundle of plywood and shingles, requiring me to make a trip to town. I'd make almost enough on the job to put the other half of the plywood bundle in my stock. This became my strategy for building inventory—overbuying to get full package pricing then put the leftovers in the store.

Taking time for another quick visit with Eddie Peter, he wanted to know how things were going. I told him. "I'm getting a lot of calls for hardware. I don't want to sell it. The town has a hardware store. But people want to get everything at one stop. They want to see a place like this where everything is under one roof."

"Are you getting any contractor business? Are the guys that use this stuff every day coming to see you?"

"No," I told him about losing the sale of a porch because I didn't have the board to make the step. "Full bundles of every size are more than I need. The packages I bought averaged costing $1,000.00. I'll get in debt over my head real quick."

Eddie got a smile on his face. "How far did you get with your $10,000?"

"It's gone. I have nice new lumber spoiling because I haven't had what anyone wanted. I'll get to use some of it on this job."

Still grinning, Eddie said, "You'd better just send them to Ranchero."

He saw a chance to make a sale. "We can help you, but like I told you. It won't be a wholesale deal. I'll treat you the best I can, but I

60

have to pay those men to process your order. We can make up some mixed packages of random length stuff."

That's what I had in mind." I said. "We're just selling a few boards at a time. That's the way I'll have to buy it."

We made a deal that he would put together small packages of sizes I didn't have, a mix from 1x4's eight feet long to 2x12's sixteen feet. He'd watch the lumber market at the time of sale and charge me fifteen cents a board foot to cover his handling. Eddie told me, "Work with the contractors. They'll make you or break you. That is where you'll build your volume. They'll expect a discount, they'll be impatient, and you may have trouble getting them to pay their bill, but you need their support to speed your turnover."

I looked out the window and recognized a pickup carrying a heavy tail load of long lumber. It belonged to a family from home and every stick of his order was a size I had in my stock. He must have seen me or my truck because he made an effort to be looking in another direction when I walked out of Eddie's office.

"Hello, George" I spoke first.

"Hi, Charlie" He wasn't as friendly as if we'd met at home.

"Have you heard that I am stocking lumber to sell now? I tried to be pleasant. You won't have to go so far if you need it."

"That's good to know. In case I didn't get enough." It was obvious he wasn't interested in dealing with me.

We kept getting calls for hardware. I was told, "It is the backbone of the business anywhere lumber is sold." There wasn't room or time in our day but everyone who came in thought we should sell hardware. The store in town was going downhill fast. Once a booming business, two changes of ownership brought it into the hands of a family who had no knowledge of building and couldn't stock the right things to get a job done. His bin of copper fittings wouldn't work on plastic pipe.

He bought the business with financial assistance of a partner who backed out and left him with substantial debts. Then he let suppliers sell him some packages that were too big for our small town. As a result he was out of the every day basics while looking at shelves that were full of dead stock. He had no way to finance the purchase of the items he needed and ran out of so many things the local cynics named his store "The Outhouse."

Eddie Peter let me push a shopping cart up and down his aisles and pick a 'little of this and a little of that' then gave me a little discount at the cash register. Then Thelma and I made a similar deal with a feed store in Silver City. If we left town we could get supplies from the North or the South.

"Get your own account. Get hooked up with a chain or franchise." The advice from customers made it sound as simple as buying a pair of shoes.

The first chain I asked didn't want to open an account unless we could purchase $750,000 in merchandise each year. Another required their dealers to buy a membership in the company. Their field representative wouldn't promise to send us a truck with less than a $5,000.00 order. Worst of all their buyers might send us an allocation of something we didn't order. I dropped consideration of them with visions of what I might do if they suddenly shipped fifteen lawn mowers.

We'd seen an Amarillo Hardware truck parked at the store in town. Thelma got a phone number from their driver. They weren't anxious to service two stores in the same small town. The one that was here was struggling and they didn't want to add to his problems. But they promised to check out my credit application.

I had a good repayment record at the bank and my gasoline credit cards were current; nothing else I could report. Dun and Bradstreet had never heard of me and I had no reasonable estimate for annual volume of sales. I left so much of that application blank I was surprised when they approved it. They assigned us a salesman who was supposed to take our order every two weeks. He appeared once every two or three months with some excuse of a broken down car or bad tires and about once a year because his wife had another baby.

Opening the hardware account was the step that made people aware we were in the business to sell things. Eventually the company sold us a big catalog so we could show people what we could order. We took a lot of abuse because we had only a few dollars available at a time. One builder was fond of coming through the door saying, "Do you have it? Or am I going to have to go to a real store?"

We left that catalog open in plain view so everyone could see what we could purchase. Their demands increased. The hardware list was endless—it branched into bolts and fasteners, seeds and garden supplies. There were calls for paint and power tools. We could add a few things with each order, like dipping into the ocean with a teaspoon. We grew a little at a time but not nearly fast enough to satisfy our community. Their demands still reflected a belief that we should have everything they wanted, now it was them rubbing that magic lamp and expecting us to grab everything as it fell out of the sky.

The building we'd designed was totally inadequate. I'd planned it as a shop—with racks to store the lumber in piles of a few boards of each size across the back. The full packages had taken all the floor space and some sizes had to be carried around or over other sizes. It was not safe for customers to be shopping for hardware beside where I was welding and the big doors I'd planned so I could bring equipment through the front were drafty and unwieldy.

My insurance agent convinced me it wasn't feasible to buy fire insurance for raw lumber. We were faced with little choice except to start construction on another building.

Cement created the greatest demand of anything we sold. We had to gear up to handle a greater volume. Everyone wanted cement and it had to be cheap. The 94 pound bags of powder that were made to be mixed with water, sand and gravel to make concrete or stucco were the most-asked for item. They were heavy, awkward and dirty to handle—easy to rip and spill—and had to be kept absolutely dry or they would turn into solid rock. When I was building homes I tried to always keep a few extra bags on hand for shortages, small jobs or just to help a neighbor.

When a lumber yard wanted to knife a competitor they dropped the price of their cement. It became a cutthroat business. They sold it below cost as bait to get people into their store at the start of a job. All we had to do when we became members of a class the cynics considered to be unregulated thieves, was to write down our price for a sack of cement. It was made and bagged at Albuquerque or El Paso where orders needed to be placed during the winter. Summer demand was usually more than the plants could supply. Stores that wanted to use it as a drawing card either built a good stockpile or ran out completely. Some who had none in stock used a very cheap and well advertised price to bring people from hundreds of miles so they could tell them, "I'm sorry. We're out." Or It's ordered," when they got to the store.

They sent their grandmothers after cement. (Illustration by Grem Lee)

Retail places who were selling it at a loss wouldn't talk to a customer who wanted a truckload for resale. The plants that made it only sent it out in semi-truck loads and no trucker was going to a destination where there was no forklift.

I had to fight my way around all that mess and spend the day in a hot, slow, heavily loaded truck to satisfy customers who wanted it for the price they saw advertised in the Albuquerque stores.

Hugh B. McKeen, used lots of cement in concrete irrigation ditches on his farm about 30 miles away, bought his cement in semi-loads, stored it in his barn and bought a small forklift to handle it. He'd sell it to me 100 sacks at a time so now I saved one hundred seventy miles when I went after more. To put it in my barn I climbed up on the back of that truck ten times and carried ten sacks to the rear. Then I got off and carried each sack-one at a time to a stack in the building. Each one had to be handled again when it was sold and some customers wanted it delivered. I charged $1.00 per sack more than my cost and they thought they'd been hijacked.

Lots of the customers were lazy, wanting everything done for them. They sent their wife or their grandmother. One man's wife was walking on crutches after crushing an ankle in a car wreck. He sent her forty miles in a little pickup covered with a camper shell for ten bags of cement. I was gone. Thelma had to call someone to do the loading and paid him ten dollars which she added to the lady's bill. The man made the next trip—mad—very mad—to tell me I was a crook and that he should have sent her to some other store. "They'd have help! They'd be glad to load it! You should keep help. It wouldn't cost you but $5.00 an hour! Some minimum wage kid is all you'd need!"

"Then I'd have to add about $100.00 to each sack to pay that kid!" I told him.
He left in a rage and never came back.

Our sales volume was never great enough to justify hiring grunt help for nothing but loading. Everyone knew I was bringing in the merchandise and taking it out, not present at the store lots of the time. They'd phone dozens of times every day asking, "Do you have it?" or "How much is it?" But it was really rare for them to ask when it would be convenient for them to come and get anything that needed my presence to handle.

I never expected Thelma or any of my women employees to load cement, it was such a popular item and customers so cost conscious we put up a sign that said $1.00 extra if Thelma loads."

One builder thought it was funny. "OK, I'll send a dump truck and tell her to earn her dollar!"

I got a call from a man who was selling cement out of Mexico. It was full loads only, 480 sacks at a time, but the price was attractive. I told him I had no forklift. "Get some help together. Get a bunch of kids! It won't take that long!" He was pushy. "The truck driver should help!"

Two customers promised to help if I'd let them have half the load at cost. I made a set of forks to go on my tractor. But its rated capacity was half the weight of a pallet of cement.

We made it through that load with everyone still alive—and not many sacks dropped or broken. This was about $2.00 cheaper than any I'd ever had before. The town's appetite was sharpened for cheap cement. That half- load was soon gone and they were begging for more.

I started shopping for a forklift. Prices started at about $15,000 for anything in running condition. I struck out in Albuquerque, and made calls to Amarillo, Lubbock, El Paso and Denver without doing any better. I didn't foresee enough profit to stay even with what it would cost me in interest. My banker said, "No" to financing equipment. He didn't want to take the chance of owning it if I went broke. The dealer finance plans were more expensive and my banker didn't want me to get spread too thin. All I could do about that dream of owning a forklift was to keep it high on my want list. Most of the time I'd worked with about $10,000.00 of his money. I'd pay up some and then borrow it back. That's all he thought he could let me have at a time on an unsecured signature loan.

There were people on the street, especially one obnoxious smart-alec from Apache Creek telling everyone I had lots of money. I should build a shopping center. They had their eyes on the loan value or market value of my ranch. That still belonged to my mother and neither of us had the authority to sell or mortgage it without the consent of the other. This also applied to my home and the new barns I was building. But these people already had their noses too deep in my business. I saw no need to explain any farther.

I ordered another load of Mexico cement.

A few of the unemployed men and teen-aged boys gave me half-hearted promises to help but none showed up. Two stout-looking men came with the truck. They were drivers for an independent hauler. They parked it and said, "You've got an hour, after that the standby time is $125.00 an hour!" They walked down to the creek and spent the time messing around a beaver dam.

The sun was hot. The trailer was 54 feet long, parked on a steep slope with the tail at the door of my shop. Two men came from town to help me. Ysidro Garcia was stout and willing but in his middle sixties. Chris Cordova had some physical and medical problems that dated back to an auto accident when he was a child. He lasted about ten minutes and quit, totally exhausted.

We could use the tractor for half-pallets. It made us handle half of the cement twice. Ysidro thought it was just as quick if he carried the top half of the pallet to the tail of the trailer and let me take it off and put it in the stack. We handled half the load with the tractor and half by hand.

There were no customers murdered near my front door that day. It is one of the few times I was ever close to that store that some wise guy didn't deliver a taunt about my "easy money."

Chapter Seven

HELP-HELP-HELP

Our retail business was still in its infancy when we learned we had to hire some help.

Even if only two customers came in a day they were there at the same time. Or one was ringing the phone while we were taking care of another but very few men would consider the minimum-wage rates we had to offer. Most of our employees were female and only a handful of them had any experience using the merchandise we sold. We had to try to explain the names and how to use every item before they could speak enough of a builder's language to sell it.

One young lady blushed, became embarrassed and refused to listen while I was giving her a lesson in identifying pipe fittings. I'd meant nothing inappropriate as I showed her a short piece of metal pipe with threads on both ends and told her it was called a 'nipple' and that inside threads were female, outside were male.

We were usually so busy we tried to use anyone who wanted to work. Very often that was the young single mothers who were also likely to be school drop-outs without any working knowledge of fractions, percent and lacking ability with the simple math they needed to work at the check-out stand. Each brought to the job the personal baggage of her own soap opera. While on our payroll they kept our phone tied up with calls to lawyers, case workers, boyfriends and babysitters.

I tried to sympathize while I trained them but our government had become so liberal with various welfare programs they had little incentive. Most of them were getting food stamps, free commodity groceries, rent subsidies and Women, Infants, and Children assistance on their medicals bills and utilities.

I stepped through my front door one day to find the phone unhooked and laying on the counter while my young employee slowly read the sizes of drill bits from a rack on the opposite side of the room. "One" pause "Eighth" pause "Three sixteenths."

"What are you looking for?" I asked, knowing the customer would become impatient and hang up mad and disgusted with the speed she was moving.

"He wants a three-quarter drill bit. I can't find it!" She was close to tears.

"Get over there on the other side of the rack!" It's about as big as my thumb!" I yelled at her as I made my way to pick up the phone. Then I asked both her and the customer, "Is he drilling steel, wood, or masonry?" This girl had put out enough hardware orders to know there were different tools for different jobs. But it was a "How much is it?" call from someone's wife and she just knew he wanted to make a hole.

This girl needed to understand fractions. I gave her a measuring tape and told her she could take it home. I slowly pointed out how each inch was divided in halves, then quarters, eighths, and sixteenths. The longer I talked the more frustrated she became. She sobbed, "But three-sixteenths just has to be bigger than three-quarters!"

When she quit she told me, "As soon as I have one more baby I'll be making more than you're paying me!"

A painful decision came when I had to fire one woman who showed up on time every day but couldn't seem to learn. I'd given her more than she could digest when I told her the names of each style of molding so I cut a few inches of each, labeled it, and glued it to a display board to keep near her cash register. It would only take her a moment to identify quarter round or door stop and sell it for the appropriate price.

A customer came back one evening carrying a pile of baseboard and his purchase receipt, "Can I return this? I got too much."

It was clean and in good condition—there was no reason not to take it back and refund his money. But the paperwork showed she had charged for base shoe, shaped similarly but ¾ inch high instead of 2 ¼ and less than half the correct price. She'd disregarded the help I'd given her so I had to let her go.

I was told that the way to avoid that kind of a problem was to put the stock on a computer with bar-code scanning at the check-out.

She wouldn't have to know what she was selling. Years passed before we adapted to that technology and it brought its own load of problems.

One elderly and partially disabled man moved his family and all his belongings to town thinking he had a job with the school. Something happened and he wasn't hired. He was desperate. He walked with a cane and traveled over a mile to get to work on a motorized wheel-chair. He couldn't help with heavy loading but he appeared honest, dedicated and had a good background in math. There was a certain consolation in knowing he wouldn't get pregnant. We would keep him busy checking incoming orders or working at the cash register. He'd hardly learned his way around the store when we got into a busy spurt where everyone was tied up with an impatient customer—the phone was ringing on two lines at once and a delivery truck driver was trying to get my attention.

"This new helper got on his wheel chair to leave. "Not feelin' good. Goin' home." He mumbled in my direction.

The next day he was on time and appeared healthy, "I just had to rest a little and take my medicine." He explained that much then rattled off some medical terminology that meant nothing to me. A few days passed and he did the same thing, again picking a moment when we were busy and feigning sickness to leave us without help. I expected no one to work if they were ill but we wouldn't have hired him if he couldn't keep a dependable schedule.

The explanation we needed came when a customer engaged our helper in a conversation about a high-school football game. He'd been getting sick and leaving at the proper time to watch his son play ball.

No person existed who could fill all positions. I enjoyed helping people with their framing layout, cement quantities or plumbing problems, all things most of our helpers were totally lost at trying to understand. But I wanted no part of anything that involved computers, cash registers and bookkeeping.

Thelma did the work of several people: She was constantly training new helpers and correcting errors when they didn't watch for price changes, wouldn't collect names, addresses and signatures for people who ran charge accounts and accepted partial payments without recording who did it. She put up with those hassles all day then sat at her desk half the night working on orders, inventory control, and the tons of paperwork involving taxes, payroll, insurance, and trying to collect from people who owed us.

The helpers came and left. Some would have worked if we paid in cash and reported nothing that could discount their early retirement check from Social Security or any of the welfare programs. I was afraid to take that bait. We were also paying for a workman's compensation insurance policy. I would have really felt foolish trying to process an injury claim for an employee who wasn't on my payroll. In the back of my mind I thought each should have felt some responsibility to contribute to the health of the business. Most could care less and only looked at the amount of their take-home-pay. Many refused to adjust the time of their lunch break or quitting time, even if they were in the middle of filling an order.

One young woman kept a Gatorade bottle in her hand most of the time. We didn't see the light until she missed work—locked up in jail on a D.W.I. charge. She'd been keeping that drink spiked with vodka.

We played on the chance to keep dependable help when our son, Jesse, found himself out of work. Some budget cutback had downsized Cannon Air Base and devastated the economy of Portales, New Mexico. Our two families combined in a joint endeavor to build up and manage the business. His schooling and experience in computerized bookkeeping brought our store into the modern world. A girl at the check-out stand no longer needed to know the name of the item she was selling—just a quick scan of the bar code brought up a description, a price, printed an invoice, and told us when to reorder.

Jesse's wife, Monica, checked in hardware orders, helped with the cleaning and worked the cash register. Our two-year-old grandson, Michael, was still in diapers but he learned the store layout and became proficient in leading customers to what they wanted to find.

President Bill Clinton declared 'War on the West,' especially grazing permittees on National Forest Land, no future remained for ranchers. I sold most of our ranch and cattle which gave us the money to finance a bigger store, larger trucks, a newer forklift, and then a more complete stock on the shelves.

We finished a big add-on room that expanded our product line from lumber and hardware to daily necessities like laundry soap, pet supplies, and notebook paper for the school kids. But those efforts were rewarded with more complaints about things we didn't have. None of our suppliers offered watch and camera batteries and we never tried to get a license for firearms or ammunition. Some customer found a reason to leave mad every day.

Those constant complaints and continual demands for more things than we could provide took the enjoyment away from any gains we could make. They played a significant role in causing several good helpers to quit. The local shopping habit never changed—buying all they could when they were out of town but expecting the local merchants to have everything they might need of whatever they forgot or ran short of. Our girl at the front was the target of a lot of abuse she had no way to control.

One lady took it all in stride and managed to keep a smile on her face through all the ranting, raving, foot stomping and screaming the most vile-tempered customers could hurl our way. Helen Milligan had done a man's work beside her husband when they worked cattle, ran a saw mill or drove a truck. She had fixed flat tires and done grease jobs when they ran a gas station. After his death she ran a trading post near Deming, and came back home to retire. But Social Security wasn't enough. She worked for us eleven years. I couldn't stop her from helping younger grandmothers load cement so I bought her a hydraulic cart that cranked up like a scissor jack.

We never had to worry about Helen being on time or staying busy when she got here. A moment with no customers would find her refilling an empty shelf or wiping the dust from something. She gave us all her energy until at age seventy-eight she had to slow down. There was no one with comparable qualities to replace her and the approaching absence of any dependable help played a major part in our decision to close the store.

Chapter Eight

MY CHECK COMES WEDNESDAY

Many people had encouraged us to sell building material so it came as a disappointment that our lumber moved so slowly. I was encouraged when I came home one day and found the stack of 2x6-12's nearly gone.

When I asked Thelma how the sale had gone she said, "I hope we get paid for them."

She explained that a young man from Texas was working for a good friend twelve miles away at Apache Creek. This owner was out of town; the carpenter ran out of lumber, and we should get paid when those folks came home. I had no reason to distrust the neighbor. Our families had been friends for 100 years. Even at that moment I had one of their farm machines parked behind my barn. They had bought it new, used it a few years and quit farming. I'd borrowed it, used it twice and quit too. Neither of us needed it. There had been no hurry to return it.

Now I needed to replace that bundle of lumber and didn't have the money to do it.

The people in this town expected their grocer, the gas station and the mechanic to let them pay when they had the money. They thought a partial payment should be sufficient if they didn't have all of what they owed.

It was a longstanding tradition. Ranchers received one payday a year when they sent their cattle to market. Loggers were out of work any time the woods were muddy. Merchants were supposed to wait until cash was available, and expected to have extra compassion and patience with anyone who had sickness, a death or any accident in their family. Cutting them some slack was the first step to pleasing them.

Some tried to just say, "Charge it" and never worried about getting anything paid for. That type of management had closed local businesses as long as I could remember. So I was determined it wouldn't happen to me. I told everyone we wouldn't be giving any credit.

This early sale, we learned, was typical of what we'd face. Workers doing a job wanted us to send the bill to someone else.

Someone must have gone down the street with a loudspeaker screaming, "Charlie gives unlimited credit!" Everyone had a different excuse for buying without paying. They had practice and experience.

"Don't you trust me?" came from people we'd known for years. They were ready to boycott us if we wouldn't let them charge.

'I don't have my checkbook' really meant, 'I don't have any money in the bank.' 'My check comes next Wednesday' may have meant a check was coming but it didn't mean we'd get any of it. "You know I'm not going anywhere" didn't cover the checks we had to write to keep our merchandise coming.

Many forgot their promise as soon as they got out the door. Thelma started sending monthly statements which were disregarded. She started adding monthly interest. This may have encouraged more unpaid accounts because it indicated we actually had a credit policy.

None of our suppliers allowed slow payment. Some would take my personal check when I loaded. Others demanded a cashier's check in advance.

In time we got more accounts established with wholesalers who required complete payment by the tenth of the month. Those slow payers delayed our progress. Many customers demanded more items and a better selection but we couldn't bring it in faster than we could pay for it.

At some counters I encountered check guarantee machines, instant electronic withdrawal from my account. This prohibited bringing something home and collecting for it while my check was on its way to the bank. Our checks had to be recorded at corporate headquarters in Amarillo, Lubbock, Atlanta or Salt Lake City on the tenth of the month. Our records were flawless but one supplier in Albuquerque refused to let me load on a Tuesday, the fourteenth. The tenth had hit on a Friday and Monday had been a holiday. The check was in the mail to their office in Phoenix but that excuse didn't work. When we experimented with cash discounts we offended the ones who were dependable and on time.

I must have had 'stupid' tattooed across the middle of my face when a trusted contractor was checking prices. He was going to build a large storage room for a neighbor lady and promised to give me the order if I could match the bid he'd gotten from a different lumber yard. I had to make some deep cuts in my prices but got it marked down to where he said, "Load it. She'll be in to pay you."

I failed to ask, "When?" Two years passed before she paid the bill. He claimed he didn't see that one coming and made some partial payments from money he made on other jobs.

After we shut off the credit for one contractor he bought the time to do another job by knowing how to play the system on a bounced check. The warnings and waiting time that was used up before the case made its way through the judicial process was slower than it would have been if we'd just let him charge it at the start of the job.

Our refusal or any limit we placed on the amount of credit brought on violent temper fits. "So that is how you show your appreciation for the business I've given you! You can bet you won't see me here again!"

After our statements were ignored for several months we sent a demand letter—"pay or face court action." Once in a while that brought a response but usually we had to file a claim which started a slow process guaranteeing some family would be mad forever. I'd pay the court costs and carry the papers to the Sheriff's office. A deputy might serve the complaint or lose it. Both the sheriff and the magistrate were counting toward votes in the next election. Once the papers were served the defendant had twenty days to answer. Some paid at this point but most knew the system. The Magistrate might wait for months before he scheduled a hearing. I never lost a case if it got to this point. Many were won by default because the person who owed the debt failed to appear in court. Often after winning, I never received any money if they had nothing I could take to pay the bill.

One hearing deserves mention because it was rare in our county for a lawyer to be serving as magistrate. He decided the case in my favor, and awarded me $250 on a $2,000.00 debt. I learned the reason a few days later. The man I sued was the landlord for the judge's father in one of their business ventures. A more complete description follows in the chapter "Neighbors by Spite."

The most difficult case to collect was against a lady who was running a café, a thriving business in the middle of town. Her payment record had been so slow I wouldn't take an order unless she promised to pay at the time of the delivery.

"I can handle it!" She screamed into the phone when I made that request.

She wanted some painted metal roofing, lumber for a porch and deck and a chain link fence around her yard. Her order came from three of my suppliers.

Her carpenter and the fence builder were anxious to start immediately if I could get the order ready.

She flagged me when we met in the road, "I have to be at the café for just a few minutes. Go ahead and unload it. I'll be back and pay you before it's all off the truck."

Her building crew helped me unload. She didn't come back. I drove to the café. Her helpers hadn't seen her. Four or five months later I added interest and filed a lien against her property.

She hired a lawyer who claimed my lien was invalid because I'd waited more than ninety days. He made me release it under a threat of a countersuit against me for harassment. A year passed and I filed a court case and won. She promised to pay $100 every two weeks. Another year went by with her making only a few inconsistent payments.

She owned a shiny blue pickup that was always washed, waxed and spotlessly clean. When she could leave her café she drove it up and down the street to see whose vehicles were parked at her competitors' places of business. I got into a conversation with one of the ladies who worked for her. "Please spread the word that I am going to carry my papers back to the Magistrate and check into what I have to do to seize that pretty truck in a sheriff's sale. I don't know how it all works, but she is in default on a court order. "I'll bid what she owes me."

"What'll you do with it? You already have two pickups. You are just too lazy to keep 'em clean."

I mentioned the name of a young man who hauled wood with the worst wrecks in town. "He owes me for my old brown Chevy pickup. He tore it up before he got it paid for. I've got a court order against him too. He ain't paid nothin'!" I'll loan hers to him and he can haul wood for me. He might get my bill paid before he ruins hers."

We shared a good laugh.

A day or two passed and the Magistrate's office called, "Come in and get your money. It is on our table."

We knew almost everyone and now we were paying for what we knew about each of them. The families were big and the neighbors clannish. Each person who got his feelings hurt spread his anger as far as he could. Every incident in which we had to use force to collect added to the mob who vowed to never again come near our store.

We fell into a routine that usually caused a cliffhanger the first week of every month. Bills came that we had to pay. Some people were dependable, paying their account without us having to send a statement. Others got the bill and waited another month, paying just in time to avoid the next month's interest. We squeaked by, sometimes with enough money to add some new stock. Too often it was with the help of money we got from some other source. In time our books showed $30,000 out—slow accounts against people we thought we could trust. Thelma got firm, telling them "You'll pay something on what you owe before you charge any more." When they said, "I don't have my billfold"—her answer was "Go home and get it." We could do nothing about the ones who skipped to Montana or Tennessee, and often learned they had done the same thing to the grocery store and the gas station. We hoped they could live with their conscience.

Our problems didn't come from the poorest people in town. The liens and court cases were against a doctor, a retired policeman, a cousin who owned several ranches, a school teacher with forty years tenure, several contractors and at least three people who ran businesses in the middle of the Village.

Nearly three years passed before I got a face-to-face meeting with the neighbor who gave me the shaft on that first bundle of lumber. He was gone a lot. He and his wife got a divorce. She stayed on a place that had come to them through her family. When I threatened court action her mother paid the bill. When I met him again it was in a bar and he'd consumed enough drinks to affect his attitude.

He asked, "How's it feel to be the only one in town with any money?"

"It lets me know who my friends are."

I hadn't planned to have to win a fist fight to help anyone. I walked away with the gut feeling I should have knocked him off that barstool.

There were other times we made friends by helping people who needed a little extra time. Aurora and Marcella Kline, spinsters from Aragon, were honest enough to ask before starting a remodeling job. They would have never comprehended the procedure to obtain a loan. Their job became bigger than either of us anticipated but they never missed a month until they paid every cent.

Many times we stayed afloat by selling cattle or with money that came from rental houses and property we were selling.

The town watched us. They laughed. They kept their noses in our business. They spread the word on the street that we were wealthy, we could find it somewhere—we didn't have to be paid.

I remember lessons from my Dad. He used a word called 'stickability.' It was a philosophy and a family virtue. He used it to mean going forward with a project when all odds were against you. We thought we were providing a necessary service and derived enough pleasure from helping a satisfied customer that we went on for years without thinking of quitting.

Chapter Nine

GROWING PAINS

Our course was set. All we had to do to build a successful business was stock everything the customers wanted, write a dirt-cheap price and let them pay when they felt like it.

Often it was embarrassing when someone needed a common every day item but we hadn't yet found the money to put it in stock. I'd been kidded when I was building my shop, "What's it going to be, an airplane hanger?" The first barn looked like a lot of space. With three drive-in doors along the front, one was for Thelma's car because neither of us liked to scrape frozen windshields in the morning. A door with twelve foot overhead clearance was in the center because I usually kept high sideboards on my truck. At the start I would take cattle to the sale and return with building material. This would be a dry place to park a load. A third door opened to my work area where I could have a roof over my head while welding or building a cabinet.

Behind the area for Thelma's car we'd partitioned a separate space for her upholstery shop and an office. She parked her car there two nights before someone filled it with old couches and chairs they wanted covered. Our plans changed daily. Space behind my work area was planned for racks to store an assortment of lumber. Never planning to stock each size in full bundles, our first order filled that area and every available inch in all our other sheds and barns.

We were being asked to sell hardware but had no place to display it. The place I'd planned for lumber was eventually cut into a separate, well insulated room for paint.

Within a few months my lumber piles had been picked over. I could have used every inch of every board by cutting the crooked pieces into blocks or bracing but no one would buy a bad board. Now I could build another barn from lumber that wouldn't sell. This time it was an open shed sixty-six feet long with divider posts and platforms to give each size of lumber its own cubicle. An overhang on the end that caught the most weather gave Thelma a place to park her car.

From someone's junk pile I scrounged some old oilfield pipe for support posts and some tubing from an amusement park that was already welded into trusses. The banker let me stay in the game with a $10,000 debt limit. He seemed satisfied when we'd make a payment, bring the interest bill up to date and borrow it back. He said, "That's what we're here for."

I tried again, dealing with the local lumber company, to fill the new shed. Their policy was to only sell to dealers, nothing but full packages, and only when the order came out to a semi-load. Yet, they were still limping along at part-capacity because demand was sour.

The salesman gave me the same answer as two years before. "I'll call you back. I'll call you right back."

In another call a few days later I got to talk to Emil Romero, a friendly man, who had cousins all around our town. He was willing to work with me but his prices were higher than I'd been paying around Albuquerque. The convenience of a shorter haul made me decide to deal with him. He demanded full payment—a cashier's check before loading—and refused to send any two by six, sixteen feet long, claiming that most needed size was always in short supply.

Dennis Swapp, who lived twenty miles away in Luna had put together an old truck that didn't have to be on the road every day. This happened before I owned a forklift so he hauled that load and left his rig at my place a few days while I handled each package a stick at a time, once from his truck to mine and again into the new lumber bins.

Dennis told me, "They were sure grouchy. The yard hands think a load is supposed to be all 2x4's or 2x6's. It's too much trouble to drive their forklift from one pile to another.

Hand-handling and getting to see each board one at a time showed me they had sent a lot of unacceptable junk. I culled it to avoid arguments with my customers. But I had to adjust my cost and what I could charge for each good board to allow for this waste. They were also wet and heavy, hadn't been close to a dry kiln. It was almost as if they were doing everything they could to make sure I never ordered from them again. I went back to the mill to complain. The man I talked to wasn't interested in public relations.

Lumber and rigid insulation.

Plumbing parts became the backbone of the business. Shown here are assorted copper, plastic, and steel parts.

Sewer and drain fittings.

Forklifts.

Regarding the water content he told me, "It is regularly checked with a moisture meter and it meets specifications."

As for the junk mixed in the packages he gave me a little handbook of rules for lumber graders. He knew which page and paragraph to turn to while he was asking, "Is it more than five percent?"

Five percent of a package of their 2x4's, 416 pieces, would be about twenty-one boards to throw away when a new bundle was first opened. "That is close." I answered.

"You don't have a thing to complain about! That is what the man that grades the lumber is paid to do!" He underlined a sentence which said a certified grader was allowed five percent error and gave me the book. There was nothing polite in his dismissal. "You come back and see me if you have a problem!"

From my construction work I'd carried an account from a plumbing contractor's supply that gave me access to anything I needed in pipe or fittings. It came in handy because plumbing problems hit people without warning, no one had any idea what he might run into when he started a job and it was a sure bet they would be anxious to finish, usually without quibbling over price.

A good assortment of pipe fittings was not to be found in the local hardware store. Upset people became happy real fast when I had what they needed to get their water on. I'd been down in the ditch doing enough of that work to help me visualize the problem and help them.

Plumbing parts quickly became the backbone of our business. New suppliers brought better prices. The things I'd bought at the contractors supply were exorbitantly priced compared to what we now gave the hardware company. It taught us we could lose money in a falling market. We couldn't put a new order of elbows in the bin for .29 cents if there were still two there at $1.36. But they often went out ten at a time—we didn't want to lose the sale of ten by displaying two that were overpriced. There wasn't much to do but bite the bullet, mark the higher priced ones down and lose $1.14. Lowering prices should have been good for our public relations but it didn't help us find dollars to pay for the next order. Nor did it stop the bitching if someone bought one that came from the contractor supply.

We built display racks for copper, galvanized and black iron, four kinds of plastic and two kinds of gas pipe. There was a thinwall sewer pipe that went in the yard and a heavier grade for inside the house. We tried to keep a complete stock of fittings for all of them.

Most customers were totally lost and their homes had been completely fouled up by inexperienced handymen who mixed and mismatched the parts from all these different kinds of pipe. I found drinking water coming into homes through a mix of garden hose, electrical conduit and duct tape. The sink drain was apt to be an automobile radiator hose slanted to a knothole in the floor. I could give advice which most people were glad to get. But there was always the risk of irritating someone if my suggestion caused them to spend another dollar. Then they'd be determined to do things their own way.

One of these offended customers was a doctor who got into a dispute with the County Commissioners over the rent he should pay for their county-owned building. He moved his practice into a hurriedly-constructed addition to his home. This was an old house on the edge of a hill. He decided to dispose of sewage by laying a pipe down to a sandy patch of farmland at the bottom. But midway through that job he decided four inch pipe was getting too expensive and asked me for a reducer to change the size to three inch.

I strenuously argued that nothing about his job was sanitary or legal or feasible. He wouldn't listen. I tried to get into medical terminology and tell him that a restriction in the flow was like cholesterol that could block a blood vessel. He got mad. He yelled in my face, "That's the way we're going to do it if I'm paying for it!"

I hated sarcasm, but thought it was appropriate to use it to win an argument with another do-it-yourself plumber. This guy started by buying a roll of black inch-an-half plastic pipe. A few days later he was throwing a tempter fit while going through my sewer fittings and toilet parts, yelling "You don't have the adapter I need." When I tried to assist him he said, "I don't need your help! I was a pipe-fitter in the mines for twenty-nine years!"

86

"But you have to hook a toilet to three or four inch pipe." I told him.

"That roll I got is big enough!" He argued.

"I'll rig it up if you insist." I told him. "But you're going to have to put EXLAX in your beans for the rest of your life!" I never knew if he finished that project.

About that time a girl walked in with a sack of plastic fittings still bearing the price stickers from a big discount store in Albuquerque. With a sweet smile she asked, "Can you trade for these? I got the wrong thing. Hers were from a store that put a sale flyer in the mail every month with 2x4 studs priced below what I was paying. Those fittings were 99 cents. I led her to my bin and showed her the same thing marked 29 cents. I sold her what she needed and gave her an extra.

Trying to be pleasant but firm I told her, "Do me a favor—when you take yours back where you bought them—take this one with you and show them prices are better out in the country."

I started trying to teach my customers they didn't always save at the big stores.

The effort to find better sources of supply led me to buying from a wholesaler in Tucson, Arizona. They had a weekly truck that went to Springerville, Arizona. It could bring almost any building materials I needed. A dealer in nearby Eagar, Arizona was helpful in letting me have the use of his forklift. They'd help transfer orders to my truck for a very nominal charge, cutting my hauling distance from two hundred miles to sixty-five.

This supplier sold Douglas fir lumber—the straightest, stoutest, boards I ever had in my hands. The appearance of fir, straight and clear, beside stacks full of knots, twisted and blue-stained pine meant I couldn't give away the older stock. But a customer wouldn't buy a twelve foot board if he needed ten. I found myself giving away pine so I could replace it with fir. I didn't know that after a few months Douglas fir would dry to be so hard it would split or bend every nail. No one wanted to take the time to pre-drill each hole. Now I had to give away this beautiful fir to replace it with pine.

A forklift became more necessary and I again spent days on the phone talking to dealers. One was kind enough to tell me where to go check out an old machine in Phoenix. This one was past twenty years old and a mechanic who serviced them had scattered parts of it all over his backyard. He promised to give it a rebuilt engine and put it in running condition, $8,000 picked up there and no warranty. It was a gamble but all I could afford. I took the chance. Maybe this would get me by a year or two while I was getting the business started.

Now that I had a forklift, I could order cement or cinder blocks by the truck load. There would be no standby charges for holding a truck too long and I'd save a lot of hard work I was doing by hand. I just hoped the old thing didn't break down and leave me in a bind.

It served me well. As the business grew we had to have smaller forklifts for the indoor work and a four-wheel drive machine for uneven ground on jobsites. Three or four others came and went but that first one was still moving material when we had our liquidation sale to go out of business twenty-five years later.

We were constantly building more barns or adding on and remodeling to get a roof over more merchandise. The same philosophy that drives a prospector to keep digging, pay dirt may come with the next shovel full, drove us to keep adding to our assortment of merchandise. We saw it as a lost opportunity each time we missed a sale because we didn't have something they needed. We'd try to have it the next time. But hindsight shows we should have hung more caution flags. Just because someone demanded something today was no assurance anyone would ever ask again. Money spent on dead stock was wasted as was the space it took to display it.

We needed clients who knew the difference between a store and a warehouse. We weren't gaining a thing if we brought it in just to put it in storage. It should sell for more than our costs and turn again and again to make the business successful. We were dealing with patrons who considered us to be criminals if we turned a profit. They wanted us to stock everything they wanted while they monitored every move of our progress with ridicule. A new shelf of merchandise, all items we had repeated calls to stock, was sure to draw the comment, "They're getting rich robbing us and flaunting their success."

More barns were built as the business grew.

Cement block.

The most helpful thing those who held that attitude could have done would have been to shut up and get out of the way. But some people stood on the sidelines and planned ways to frustrate us.

We watched a job progress from the ground breaking until the roof was finished; built by people who had always been friendly but had some reason for not spending a dollar with us. They were obviously stretching every cent—you could see them out working together when he could get away from his job. When he couldn't be there, she was hauling their material in a little two-horse trailer tied onto a mini-van. When they needed framing lumber she piled the studs over the front manger and out the tailgate. It was so small they stuffed rolls of insulation to the roof and she still had to make several trips. Month after month their job went on, using things we had in stock at competitive prices. We wondered why we should bother to make things convenient for people who went to such an effort to avoid us.

Then near the completion they brought a list for bid comparisons. They needed custom made cabinets, carpets and floor tile. These were all things that would come from the biggest stores or specialty dealers. We could only guess their motives. Was it a slap in the face? Had they finally learned the cost of so many miles of driving to haul small loads? Or, as we so often learned, were they out of money and trying to trap us in a scheme to combine low prices and local convenience with long-term credit.

Chapter Ten

PROGRESS?

Our old spotted dog greeted customers at the front door of our store for fourteen years. His floppy ears and sleepy eyes suggested some hound lineage; the rest of him was a back-alley mix that had to include some Blue Heeler. Everyone got to know him, and knew "Troubles" was his name. So friendly no one could resist him, women brought him home-baked cookies. Construction workers opened their lunch buckets and found slices of bologna or cans of Vienna sausage. A truck driver developed a routine of ordering a steak at some café before our stop. He saved the bone then made that dog climb the steps of the truck and turn with his front feet braced on the mirror arms to get his treat. Troubles learned to recognize the sound of the approaching Freightliner. One day we heard the sudden hiss of air brakes. A substitute driver almost ran over him. Then he hollered out the window, "Call off your dog!" Troubles was on his usual trip up the side of the cab. "He stopped me and now he won't let me out!"

I had to tell him, "He makes a lot more friends than I do. The weekly run of that hardware truck had reshaped our business. From builder's hardware, we expanded our line of merchandise to include paint and power tools. Then we added household cleaning products, veterinary supplies and some of the things the artists and hobbyists wanted. But my aim of helping my neighbors, by running a small place with a stock of the basic necessities, to save them a trip out of town was cultivating more hatred than gratitude. Every time someone opened the door or rang the phone we could add to the list of what someone considered basic. It was pump leathers and two-inch galvanized pipe for the man who was fixing a windmill. A bear trapping biologist needed small swivels and eighth inch cable. We could find most of those things in the hardware catalog and sell them if they could wait until the next week. The temper fits came from those people who wanted everything immediately.

Some customers didn't want to reveal the reason for their purchase. There were people who bought an elbow from the flared brass fittings but nothing compatible to go with it. Then that bin came up empty several times without those items going by the checkout stand. When the sheriff's department came to the County Fair with a display of confiscated drug paraphernalia we learned that elbow was also a ready-made pipe for smoking marijuana.

Then there was a young lady, also shopping in the flared fittings, who unabashedly told us, "I don't know what you call them, but the ends look like a puppy dog's peter."

We took lots of time, and enjoyed working with the ones who were courteous. I often had to buy a case to sell one or two items. If there was a reasonable chance someone else would ask for the remainder it was a way to stock our shelves with the things people required and often caused us to spend more than we would collect. It kept me busy building display racks and shelves or rearranging things to let people see the new items.

We used the same strategy with plywood, roofing, insulation and all the things that went together to make a house. We welcomed an order for most of a pallet. The leftovers gave us the assortment we needed to take care of the customers who only wanted a few pieces. But we had to keep building more barns to store each new item. Any profit we made was tied up in those remnants we were holding for the chance to sell to the next person. We stretched the $382.00 a month that was coming from the home I'd sold. I continued to pick up small jobs, but hunger would have come to the family if we weren't on a ranch and growing our own food.

All the heavy items like lumber, plywood and cement came from Albuquerque but my equipment was worn out. I was hauling with a twenty-six year old truck, built to haul cattle and most of the time rigged with high sideboards that had to be removed for anything that would be handled with a forklift. I'd resurrected it when it was three years old, the cab crushed flat and the glass knocked out from an accident. But at that time there were only 23,000 miles on the odometer. Rated as a 1 ½ ton, we'd lengthened the frame, put on a longer bed and made it look like a two-ton rig. Most trips it brought home five tons or more. That truck was inadequate so it really helped when John Holliday offered to help me get the supplies. He gave me the best deal I ever had on freight with trucks that hauled the lumber from Reserve, N.M. to Eagar, Arizona, they passed the town of Alpine. So he named his business Alpine Trucking. He had started with one truck and built a fleet, giving a display of empathy for small business owners who were pulling themselves up by their own boot straps.

After the lumber went through the planer and dry kiln at Eager, he hauled it again to wholesalers and lumber yards at Albuquerque. A truck going down the road empty wasn't making him any money so he gave me half-price hauling when I could order something for a back-haul. He even let his drivers put my load together at two or three pickup points, mixing lumber, steel products and cement on the same trip. Other truckers added $50.00 for each stop.

About this time a new bridge was being built on Forest Road #141 right beside the Reserve sawmill. The contractor sent a man to me with a $100.00 bill in his hand. "We need a lot of lumber for forms and braces." They told us you are a lumber dealer." He handed me the $100.00. This is yours. All you have to do is make a phone call. Place our order in your name. You won't have to touch a board. We'll handle it. We just need a dealer's name on the invoice."

I handed his money back. "They won't sell to me either." I explained my bad experiences with Stone. "I'll call them." I told him. "It won't cost you anything. But I have to get my lumber out of Albuquerque."

"See what you can do." He handed me a list that would nearly load a truck.

The next day I made my calls and took the results to the job. "It's like I told you. I can buy it cheaper in Albuquerque." Then I pointed across to the mill yard. "See that brown truck loading over there. We'll have to work with their schedule. But they'll be the ones that haul it."

"If you're going to do that, see what you can do on this plywood." The foreman was busy, keeping his eye on several machines that were running at the same time. Before I left he'd given me another list that more than loaded a truck.

I looked it over for a few minutes and got his attention. "These 2x6's here—you've put down 100 ten foot and 150 twelve feet. If they come from this company there will be 128 in a package. I'll have to trade leftovers back and forth with my stock."

"Oh that's ok." He wasn't concerned. "Just make it a bundle of each. I just ordered what we can use next week. If you treat us right there'll be another order when that's gone."

"Does the same thing work where you've written down 100 sheets of plywood? I think you'll get 44 or 46 in a bundle."

"Get me plenty. Make it three bundles."

When I took that order, I was planning to take my forklift to the jobsite for the unloading. But there were bigger and better machines across the fence working for the sawmill.

I approached the mill foreman, asking about the chance of hiring them to do my unloading. His answer was, "If those Alpine Trucks bring your load in, we'll have to get it off before we can send our stuff out. It won't take long. Don't let any of my bosses know." He paused, "If it should be late evening I don't want to have to pay my operator any overtime. But he'll probably help you for a six-pack."

"That sounds more than fair." I told him.

"Just wait 'till he's away from this yard before you give him the six-pack."

Orders for that bridge job came steady, week after week. We didn't need the forklift. The contractor handled the unloading with a crane. Some of the lumber was stamped to identify it as coming from mill number 195, Eager, Arizona. It had originated within one hundred yards of where it was being used, but traveled on trucks for five hundred miles before it came back to the customers at a cheaper price than I could have bought it when it was sixty-five miles away.

The boss appreciated the service I gave him and told me I was saving him money, giving him fresher material and cutting down on waste when I encouraged him to pay in bundle quantities. He especially enjoyed the connection we'd made with Alpine Trucking and the savings that came from not having to keep his truck and driver on the road.

By the end of that job I'd gotten far enough ahead to buy my own new truck. It looked like I was getting just what I needed when I picked a four-wheel-drive, flatbed, one-ton dually. Then came two gooseneck trailers—a flatbed for building material and a stock trailer for the ranch work. It gave me versatility. The flatbed truck design could be loaded with a forklift to deliver a pallet of cement or cinder blocks. In just a few minutes I could change trailers to move livestock or building material.

I increased my efforts to get larger orders so I could buy cheaper and sell cheaper. But with only a few people living in the trade area they would have to be loyal customers who gave repeat orders. I would have to please them with my service or I couldn't expect them to keep coming back.

This one satisfied customer had given me the boost needed to launch a new business. He wasn't bashful about telling me I'd saved him money and trouble. His attitude was a total contrast from that of a cynical town that had watched those events unfold and claimed my lack of competition had let me screw each of them and that contractor. They thought my new truck fell out of the sky for my reward. Jealously and intolerance drove them to spend their money traveling to the big chain stores where the profits would go to stockholders they would never see.

John Holiday was a friendly voice on the phone that helped me a lot. I never met him until one of his drivers had an embarrassing accident near my front door. My road was not designed for unfamiliar drivers in big trucks during the middle of the night. This man didn't swing wide enough to get his trailer to follow around a sharp curve that circled a pond. The result was a trailer twisted on its side and a load of cement lost in the water. That day John Holiday was anything but friendly.

That new bridge was built with Forest Service money from the sale of timber and it was supposed to improve the road for more logging. Very few trees were ever hauled across it. The next chain of political events stopped the sale of timber to protect the Mexican Spotted Owl. This bird was given protection as an endangered species only because he was a cousin of an owl in Oregon who the environmentalists thought was endangered.

Holiday truck accident.

Our logging industry was shut down, the sawmill closed. One hundred families had to find some other way to make a living. John Holiday sold his trucks. It looked as if the town would die and there would be no need for my store.

Our mountain scenery and quiet lifestyle was attractive to people who wanted to come here to retire or build summer homes. Surprisingly our business continued to grow. One small group of customers saw the value of finding some of their needs close to home. They appreciated what we were doing—had smiles on their faces while we were helping them—and we put all our energy into fulfilling their demands.

I found myself hauling Canadian lumber to a sawmill town. The one-ton truck soon was no longer adequate and I had to buy a bigger one. This time I raised the money by selling cattle and the grazing permit on the National Forest. It was a result of President Bill Clinton's war on the West. He and his Secretary of Interior, Bruce Babbitt, gave us eight years of constant attack as they tried to bring in endangered species, raise grazing fees, close roads and turn the Western states into a Wilderness.

We resigned ourselves to taking the bitter with the sweet. No business, no job and no occupation would ever be problem free. This retail venture showed us the potential to some day make us a living. It was close enough to our family ranch that I could sneak away and take care of the few remaining cattle without burning a tank of gasoline to get to a job everyday. My sons were getting good training in ranching, agriculture, and learning to build barns.

We had to adapt the business to fit the needs of the town. The loss of John Holiday's truck left little choice but running to Albuquerque each week to get the things we sold. We soon outgrew the second truck, a small Mack, and bought a small semi. This time it was pulled by a Kenworth. It brought the need for a commercial driver's license and D.O.T. permit. Customers were always in a hurry. It would nearly always be for something they forgot or didn't get enough of when they made their own order from the city. If we didn't have it in stock we could usually make a sale if we could tell them it would be here in a few days. No one wanted to wait until we could fill another big truck.

Our own motives were trying to build up the variety of our stock and speed the turnover. We liked to help people and definitely handled a lot of the merchandise very cheaply in an unsuccessful effort to stop the bitching.

My policy was to always bring home a full load, by figuring out the weight of every order then adding something that was cheap but heavy. It beat running half-empty. Pre-mixed concrete was a favorite, a product that was in constant demand but too heavy to pay the fuel bill if it was the only thing on the load. I also watched for every chance to add something like railroad ties or road culverts to the items we offered for sale.

Premixed concrete and irrigation pipe on my truck.

The town's attitude seemed to be controlled by a group of faultfinding cynics who kept their noses in everyone's business and thought they were performing a community service each time they found a reason to offer their criticism.

The more our business grew the more hectic our lives became. We were caught in the middle of our own whirlwind and watched it grow into a tornado. The first priority had to be the accounts we owed with panic day always coming just before the tenth of the month. We gave up trying to get everyone to pay us by then—often sending out our checks, covering what we owed, and praying someone would pay us and we could get the money to the bank before our checks bounced.

People stretched an extra month out of a convenience account. Contractors waited until their job was finished—then they expected us to keep on being patient while they waited on inspectors for an approval. Subcontractors assumed we could finance portions of several jobs at the same time but still keep the shelves full of everything anyone needed.

Someone had to stay near the phone for the "How much is it?" calls. It was a legitimate question, one I always asked before I bought anything. But it should have been asked when there was a reasonable intention of making a purchase. Half of the people who called to ask, "How much is it?" had already bought their order elsewhere. They were checking to see if they saved any money. Often our helper who answered the phone cost us the sale by not asking, "How many do you need?" A person who needed a full bundle of lumber would be quickly turned off by our price of a single board.

We worked hard to correct the assumption that we were taking advantage of our lack of competition and gouging people with our prices. Our hardware catalog stayed wide open in plain view so everyone could see what the suggested retail price of every item had been when that page was printed. For those who wanted a further explanation we showed them we used a pre-printed sticker that came with the order, with many items marked down lower, like putting stamps on mail. If our help knew a shovel handle from a paint brush they could price an order.

When customers found a difference between two stores it could very well reflect how long that item had been on the shelf. If it was plastic the price rose and fell with the oil market. A few dollars change in the price of a barrel of oil would show up on the next week's order of pipe fittings. That didn't keep someone from ringing our phone at 2:30 a.m. wanting to know a price. My disgust was surely obvious in the tone of my voice when I answered. "If it was business hours and I was in the store I could answer you!"

"If you don't want to sell it I'll find someone who does!" He hung up.

The antics of some customers provided our humor and entertainment. There was a preacher who became fascinated with a Ridgid calendar. This tool company featured photos of a beautiful, but scantily clad, young woman each month. She usually posed in some position that a plumbing tool blocked the view of the most interesting portions of her anatomy. Each time that preacher came to our store he took that calendar off the wall and entertained himself a page at a time admiring the scenery. He saw my smile one day, looked up from the September page and asked, "When's Easter?" Another time he was observing a girl in a wintry scene and exclaimed, "Well I'll be darned. Christmas is in December!"

We gave the best price we could. It had to be more than our cost and that never meant some other dealer hadn't found a better deal. But I always thought we were fighting more prejudice and misinformation than fact.

The traditional building product in our town had always been rough, green lumber straight out of the sawmill. Tons of extra weight and more shrinking and warping were always tolerated because surfaced lumber was not made here; considered to be too expensive to use. After Stone shut down their big sawmill two of my best friends put in small operations to handle the local demand. I never considered either of them to be competitors. Our products were as different as a flour mill is from a bakery but they had waiting lines, couldn't keep up with the demand and sold all the lumber they could cut for fifty cents a board foot. Mine spoiled in the stack and had to be discarded at thirty-five cents because of the local concept that surfaced lumber cost was too high.

The same shopping habit extended to wood burning stoves. A luxury item in the cities, the dealers who sold them enjoyed a good mark-up price. In our area they were a staple, everyone heated their homes with firewood. I bought some stoves for around $700.00 from an Albuquerque dealer. He had display models on his showroom floor and a young blonde saleslady with high-heeled shoes and a short skirt, who was getting close to $2,000.00 for a model I couldn't move for $900.00. Some local people who had walked by my stoves, bought from her then came back to me for a piece of stovepipe. I wasn't going to wear heels and a skirt to sell a stove.

Prices were going up for everything we sold. Twenty-five percent more that we paid was often not enough to buy it the next time but we kept on taking our responsibilities seriously, seldom closing for funerals, rodeos or any of the times there was a community gathering. Someone's pipe might break or a lost bolt could stop a machine and shut down a whole job.

Just the fact we were trying to be friendly and helpful made us a target for hostility. Some people derived their pleasure from being grumpy, sarcastic and impossible to please. Those couldn't even make friends with our dog dozing at the front door. They saw more barns and merchandise and proclaimed us to be wealthy. Without a chance to view our invoices or operating expenses they voiced opinions that we got rich robbing everyone. We were shunned and condemned but all of them were glad we were here if they had an emergency. It was hard to see how we offended so many by trying to help them.

If a stranger came we had to wait and see if he would be helpful or slap our face. The big necessity one day could turn into dead stock the next.

One carpenter was keeping a crew busy building roofs over mobile homes. He bought everything somewhere else because I had no 4x4's but promised to let me bid if I'd stock them. I bought a bundle, $1,500.00 and no one but him using them. He did one more job, used twelve posts and moved to Arkansas. Now I owned eighty-four high priced timbers which quickly warped, twisted and cracked in the pile. Customers selected a few of the best and the rest never sold.

We lost some sales because the word hadn't gotten around. People hadn't learned what products and services we could offer. But one person who had been aware of our every move was our banker. It was painful to see him ignore us when he put up two new office buildings in the middle of our town, and pay a large sum to a lumber yard in Socorro to haul every piece of the material over one hundred and thirty miles. His contractor came to my store, pushing his way in front of other customers, asking me to thread a piece of pipe.

I told him he'd have to, "Wait a minute and look around. I sell a lot of the things you're using on that job."

Already impatient, he turned indignant, "I can't buy from you. It'll mess up my deal with Raks."

Our bank was a branch of one in Socorro. And I'm sure this banker also had his finger in the loans that financed the bigger store in his town. But I think the manager of our branch should have looked out the window, seen those Socorro trucks, and told his boss to give me a chance at the bid.

Chapter Eleven

BANNED FOR BAD MOUTHING

In the advice session with Eddie Peter when I first began selling building material, he asked, "How many people live out there?" and almost as if answering his own question he'd said, "If your town gets behind you."

I now see that he knew exactly from where he was coming and where I was going. I was gambling all I had and all I would ever make on a temperamental clientele who were watching for every opportunity to undermine any foothold I might establish.

My twenty years of home building had been to subsidize a failing ranch. Then I got into stocking building material to make more efficient use of my time where I worked. I had a strong desire to be helpful but customers checked price tags and reached their own conclusions.

If one wanted to have me build a porch, I considered it to be advantageous to have the framework and roofing on hand, ready to start the job. The customer attitude was "not if any part of the cost is cheaper somewhere else." If I sold both material and the labor they saw it as double dipping. Some scornfully offered to pay for my gas if I went to a different store. It was an effort to get my day's work and the use of my truck for nothing. My stock for resale dried up the calls I was getting to use it.

We were on a rocky road trying to deal with most of the contractors. They would purchase a ten thousand dollar order somewhere else, then want an exact match on brand, price and color if they needed a few pieces to finish the job. There were, however, enough friendly customers to make us keep trying. We'd have been happier if we could run off the bad and keep only the good ones. But better deals would come to us if we could turn more volume. We put up with a lot of unnecessary nonsense.

One smart-aleck contractor managed to convince everyone he was the best to ever come to the county. Retired and from a military background, he appeared to be expecting us to salute him every time he came in the door. Other customer's attitudes showed us he was trying to destroy us. Some who had been friendly for years suddenly turned hostile as soon as they hired him. He shopped where the big box stores were a block apart and cherry-picked the best deals from each. Despising our small selection, he often smirked, "Wish I could win the lottery! It would be fun to shut you down."

He could have just stayed away, but he derived enjoyment from continual harassment, like ringing my phone at 6:00 a.m. on a Sunday morning. "I need to get this car going today." He told me. "I'll send my daughter. Give her the four bolts to put a water pump on a Subaru Brat."

"Does she know what she needs?" I answered. "They're probably metric. I don't have much in automotive parts."

"I don't know what we did with them. I thought you'd know! You should!" Anger was rising in his voice.

"You need a dealer with a good parts book." I told him. "You need to know the length, the diameter and what kind of thread is on them. They might have a special head."

His voice became more caustic. "You really think you're doing us a favor with that sorry little store! If you'd get out of the way someone might put in a good one!"

Though every visit he made was an obviously pre-planned slap in the face he was soon running several crews and I saw a potential for a lot of business if I could get along with him. When he was looking at my electrical supplies and complaining about not finding the right brands of circuit breakers I plainly told him, "I'm not an electrician and I don't know what you need. I've just got a few dollars to spend at a time. It has to be on basics. Those you see fit Square D, Westinghouse, General Electric and some of those common brands."

He screamed in my face, "That's your trouble! Trying to get rich quick! You need to stock what people need! You have no Zinsco—no Federal Pacific! You're making people sit in the dark and the cold because you're too stingy to stock something that might not sell tomorrow."

I could have ordered brooms or mops or dog collars, something a lot of people wanted but I bought a few Zinsco and Federal Pacific breakers. They were several hundred dollars of investment and he was the only builder who had ever asked for them. They didn't sell and the clear cellophane packages turned yellow. Years later another electrician wryly suggested I might peddle them in an antique store. He said, "Those brands haven't been used for thirty-years."

The same contractor was fond of telling everyone my prices weren't competitive. He'd get them a better deal. He was taking orders for painted metal roofing from one company and I for another. One day he asked me my price per square foot.

"Forty-eight cents, premium grade, 29 gauge, delivered to the job." I told him, knowing I'd got low bid on several orders.

"I've got you beat," he sneered. "I'm doing it for forty-two."

Soon after that I got an urgent request to bring a forklift to town and unload a truck. This happened a few minutes before sundown on a cold winter evening. My old forklift had no cab, no heater and no lights. This wasn't a job to take for pleasure.

I found this contractor standing with his hands in his pockets and acting innocent while his roofing customer and a truck driver argued about the price of hauling. The customer claimed the estimated freight charge was $250.00 while the driver was demanding $750.00 before he could allow it to be unloaded.

I had to irk them both with, "This forklift would have been free if I'd sold the roof."

This builder was so anxious to tear me apart that he'd lied to his customers to the tune of $500.00 to turn an order, misleading them with the price of the metal when it left the factory seven hundred miles away.

We were trying to save our neighbors a trip out of town. It was ludicrous to expect us to match the price of any big store but we watched many shoppers mislead themselves by going to where the price was the cheapest. They wouldn't do the simple math to find out what it was costing them. One passed me on the highway, shoved an arm out his pickup window and gave me a contemptuous one finger salute. They spent a day and $50.00 on fuel to bring home a $200.00 load, the fuel alone adding 25% to the cost of their merchandise. Though we brought our prices as low as possible we inspired preachers to give sermons that denounced greed, school teachers built economics lessons around price tags and lack of competition and the loafers who hung around the coffee shops or government offices had a field day condemning everything we did.

To get to our business location, on a ranch, a mile from town—half of that along a dirt road—people had to be looking for us to find us. Most came after getting directions from someone along Main Street but the people they were most likely to encounter weren't driven by any desire to be helpful. Strangers came expecting to be robbed or raped.

We recognized the vehicles of all the steady customers. When we saw them coming we knew which would be trying to stir up a fight and which would lead to a pleasant transaction. Some were so repulsive we didn't want to be bothered with their bullshit. Eventually I painted a sign, "Banned for Badmouthing" over the names of the four most obnoxious individuals and hung it on a gate at the entrance of our property.

A local newspaper ran a photo of the sign, yielding more effect than I'd anticipated. Most of the town turned out to look. I had to take it down when someone added the names of people I didn't know. Two of the men I'd banned came around with half-hearted apologies but there was no way to change their attitudes. I had to run each out of the store again. One stayed away but watched for chances to show off in public by coming through a crowd and telling everyone he wanted to shake my hand. The fourth man had a Forest Service job and made it his life's work to dominate his co-workers. He had a "mad at the world attitude" and stayed angry at me. People he worked with were pleased and congratulated me for years.

That sign caused a bunch of people to come around and express their appreciation for what we were doing. Some put us on their Christmas list for homemade cookies and candies. Others had to see how much aggravation they could get away with.

We stayed away from ballgames and other public activities. They had become a place for hecklers to yell across a room to ask for a loan or complain about a price. But a family who moved here from Oklahoma brought tears to my eyes when they invited us to their back yard for fresh-fried catfish. We'd been slapped and slandered so many times we thought there was no kindness left in the town.

Chapter Twelve

THE HONOR ROLL

So much of our effort went into overcoming the effects of a few bad tempered customers it was easy to overlook the good ones. Whether their orders were large or small we considered them good if they could use something we sold, paid for it and left without a string of complaints. Some were here several times a week others only seldom, those good ones provided incentive and finances for us to keep moving forward.

A few were so outstanding they deserve special mention. I have to put Chuck Montgomery at the top of the list when I pick out those I remember the best.

Chuck was a plumber who sold his business in Texas, moved here and built a nice home for a place to retire. His wife suddenly had a heart attack. He was overwhelmed by medical bills. His dream fell apart and savings disappeared.

Chuck established his own accounts with suppliers. But plumbing is a business that is full of surprises. It is critical to have access to all of the right parts. One little insignificant missing component can cause a family to freeze or go thirsty. It took all both of us could stock to keep his business moving.

We tried to open our doors before eight o'clock every morning. Always impatient, Chuck was usually on the front step, drinking from a thermos of coffee and petting our dog by 7:15. He knew where to find everything. We let him pull off the price tag and bar code, drop it at the checkout stand and be on his way. We trusted him and he trusted us. He'd be here fifteen minutes earlier than usual the day after he received our monthly statement. His check would be made out in full and he'd still be on his way in a minute.

Another of the best was Dave Manzi. I tried to discourage him when he asked if he could open a charge account. He was a friendly young contractor, always cracking jokes and sure of himself. I told him, "I don't want to take you to court."

"You won't have to." He was calm but persistent.

I kept stalling.

"I've been down that road too many times. I don't want to start again. Builders all start out sure and confident but unforeseen problems come up. They were too optimistic when they started the job. They didn't have enough money coming in at the end. We are the first to be pushed to the back burner. Ugly scenes always follow. They ignore our monthly statements, hang up on our phone calls and try to get by with partial   payments. Some try to bail themselves out on the next job but that repeats the problem."

"I told you, you won't have trouble with me."

Very reluctantly I let Manzi open a small account which became one of the best investments I ever made. He stayed busy turning out high quality work and gave me sizable orders. With him it was not necessary to be adversaries to buy or sell and he never gave us any problem with collections. He avoided any appearance of collusion, not even allowing me to buy his lunch when we met in a café. Then he added to the friendship by coming onto my ranch with Sue, his equally friendly wife for picnics, hikes, and campouts when they took a day off.

Dave brought to town another contractor, Jim Rockwell, who was just as friendly and honest. He was also a pleasure for us to serve. Some times Manzi and Rockwell worked together. Usually each went his own way. As these words are being put on paper, Rockwell is in a battle with cancer and not able to take on new projects.

I have to look at Manzi and Rockwell and say, "They did their part." They gave us large or small orders when it was something we could handle and neither of us complained when they could find a better deal else where. If we'd had more customers with their attitude, the final chapter of this book would have had a completely different ending.

No greater display of integrity ever came our way than the purchase of an order of rolled plastic by logging contractor, Jimmy Kellar. Calm, soft spoken, but absolutely and unquestionable scrupulous— he fought to stay in business when politics to protect the spotted owl stopped logging and closed sawmills all over the West. He had to move his equipment to the forests of New Mexico, Arizona and Colorado to go where he could find work. So it was cause for him to rejoice when he got a contract to clear the brush from under a power line close to home.

At times forest fires had shut off the electricity that flowed through those lines, the supply for Tucson, Arizona. This job was to clear, then pile for burning anything flammable below them. Some environmental regulation regarding spread of a bark beetle made him wrap those brush piles in plastic. He gave me large orders for the rolls of plastic. I bought all my hardware supplier had in stock. He ordered more. I made the rounds of my suppliers in Albuquerque and purchased all they had. Then Jimmy gave me a still larger request, one that would be a special order for the wholesaler in Albuquerque. It would take a month for them to get it.

They called back worried, "Make sure that is an order that won't be returned. We'd never sell that much if we had to stock it."

Jimmy said, "Bring 'er on."

The month passed and I told him I had his load of plastic.

He told me, "I don't need it now. The nesting season has passed for the bark beetle and they aren't requiring it." He didn't wait for me to get worried before he said, "I ordered it. I'll take it. We'll put it in my garage. Someone might need it."

Most of the contractors I dealt with would have jumped at the opportunity to pocket a few thousand dollars and let me eat that order—not Jimmy Kellar— he was a man of his word.

Another equally honest contractor was Dennis Swapp. He lived twenty miles away in Luna, N.M.-- but had a job in the Phelps-Dodge Copper Mine at Morenci, Arizona where he used tons of welding steel. I seldom saw him face to face; the orders came by phone. I'd deliver them to his yard, use his forklift, fold the bill and put it under a rock in the seat. I never worried. The next time Dennis came home he would send me a check.

The steel orders kept getting larger. I told him, "I appreciate your business, but you can buy just as cheap as I and you have trucks and trailers of all sizes. After I unload at Luna you have to load and haul over 100 miles of mountain road to get it to Morenci. Why do you mess with me?"

"Why let a man sit in a truck when I need him somewhere else?" He answered. "I can't get enough dependable help. If I send him down the road I have to worry about what he runs over." That statement showed wisdom beyond most customers who would try to haul the material to build a whole house with a Japanese pickup.

A time came when Dennis's order would cost me over ten thousand dollars. My account where I bought the steel was C.O.D. They'd been cautious about taking checks. Their secretary's cubicle was covered with checks that had bounced. Every time I paid out I kidded her about giving her some personalized wallpaper and she'd answer with "Hasn't yet." Her tone indicated they wouldn't let it happen but once.

For that order, I told Dennis, "I have to write a check before I load and I don't keep that much money in the bank." Prices were too unstable and supplies too uncertain for him to pay me in advance.

"Patty (his wife) gets over that hill in thirty minutes, unless she gets in a hurry." He answered. "Is that quick enough?"

"Sure."

"I'll leave a signed check with her."

The deal was settled. I told the secretary, "I'll get paid and the check will be good as soon as I get it off the truck." She let me load.

Customers didn't have to be big spenders to get on our honor roll. Frank Davila made it with a single trip and the purchase of a $6.00 plastic bucket. He lived two hours away in the North end of the county and years often passed between the times we saw each other. We met at the Pie Town Festival and he asked if I'd received his check.
"I didn't know you owed me anything. My wife handles the books." I told him.

"Yes, I went in your store and bought a plastic bucket." He explained. "When I got home I found I had two buckets. One was pushed inside the other. I decided I could use two of them and they were marked the same price. I sent the same amount as the first." Thelma remembered the check, a similar note of explanation, and no invoice in the files to match it. Such honesty from a customer was rare.

Shoplifting was a daily problem and one of the best aspects of using the computer to track inventory was the way it showed us how much we were losing. Any stock check of small items that could be hidden in pockets, purses or a diaper bag showed shortages. A favorite tactic was for customers to come in bunches. One would ask a question or need help finding something, anything to create a distraction while the rest of the party helped themselves.

Our candy aisle must have been irresistible. When we swept the floor we'd find empty wrappers discarded among the horseshoes. Sometimes they left half-packages of cookies on the shelf. We were helpless to prevent those problems. The monetary value of a candy bar didn't justify keeping a helper stationed there to watch every customer.

They even carried off three out of a litter of four kittens a lady had given me when I tried to raise my own mousetraps. They were cute, easily caught, and irresistible for the few days they spent on our place. Everyone played with them. But soon they weren't there any more.

One old fellow almost got away with ten steel fence posts though he had to carry an oxygen bottle to breathe. At a time we were closed, he pleaded on the phone, "I've just got to get this fence built. I can get help on Sunday, but I need thirty-five posts. Can you help me?"

"Come on in." I told him.

While I loaded his posts he apologized for not being able to help—thanked me profusely for opening up, and conspicuously fondled a roll of $100.00 bills in his shirt pocket.

When I'd finished loading I had to go to a nearby barn and get the clips that fasten wire to the posts. He was nimble enough to get ahead of me, find Thelma inside the store and pay her for twenty-five posts. I caught the mistake and made him correct it before he drove away.

It showed me customers were watching for a way to cheat and made me all the more appreciative of the honest ones who politely pointed out mistakes we made in which we would have cheated ourselves.

Chapter Thirteen

FIGHTING MY GOVERNMENT

As money came in from the sale of the ranch we spent it building a bigger and better store. It made economic sense to get out of a business that wasn't paying its own way and reinvest in one that appeared to hold some potential. Tax laws gave us strong incentive as money from real estate could be spent on a building and dollars from cattle could convert to more merchandise.

We added twenty feet to the front of our building and modernized the entrance, making it look like a store instead of a workshop. Then we increased the quantities we were carrying of most major lines of building material. We wanted to be able to fill larger orders when they came our way. I couldn't sell cheaper but I had it where it was convenient. The big stores in the city could tear each other apart with their price wars.

The payments that came from the sale of the ranch were sporadic as buyers wanted to play cowboy but couldn't afford it. Three new owners came and went. They'd get behind, we didn't want to repossess so we would wait. The next buyer would put enough money into the deal to catch up on our payments. Now things had turned around. A business that had been started to subsidize a failing ranch was being propped up by the money that came in from the sale of that ranch.

There seemed to be no end to the things that we could sell if we had them when someone needed them. The satisfaction and smiles of those who traded with us drove us. School supplies, wedding gifts, birthday cards—no other hardware store should have been expected to carry such an assortment. We got calls because they had no other place to go. Then people from Silver City, Magdalena and Safford, Arizona exhibited habits of getting mad at their hometown suppliers and coming to us just as our neighbors had gone to their towns.

Many of the people who owed us money were honest, just slow. As they got around to paying us we had a cash flow that kept us going. Our growth and restocking schedule were delayed to suit their whims—most stayed with their shopping habit of going to the bigger stores when they got their paycheck. We were still expected to have anything they needed on short notice, especially when they were short of cash. Stocking for those small orders kept us going around the same old monotonous circle. If we had to pay more we'd have to charge more. The price tags we wrote would only satisfy a few of them.

A solution seemed to come when we signed a deal with Promotions Unlimited, a company headquartered in Racine, Wisconsin. Their business plan was to give a small store a line of merchandise whose pricing was competitive with the big box retailers. It was a traffic builder to bring more customers through the door.

Canned groceries and household goods came with Ben Franklin Franchise.

They had a monthly sale in which daily necessities like toilet paper, dish soap and paper towels were at rock bottom prices. There were also specials on costumes and candy to fit whatever holiday, like Halloween or Valentine's Day, came that month. The prices we received barely covered the cost of the merchandise. We had to make up the cost of postage to mail the flyers and all the storage and handling costs from other things people bought.

The Promotions Unlimited contract led into a Ben Franklin Franchise when the two companies merged, giving us a source of supply for a lot more of the things our customers wanted. We added another large room and committed ourselves to a minimum order of $2,500.00 each month.

From one of the Promotions sales we purchased a few cases of canned peaches at a price that we could turn and stay below grocery chains. This wasn't an item anyone would expect to find in a hardware store but something almost anyone could use. They didn't sell. Thelma parked a shopping cart filled with peaches beside the front door with a big poster to show the price. People would stand there with a hand on that cart and tell us, "I'd buy more from you if you'd get your prices right." We enjoyed a few peach cobblers then she had to discard them because we'd held them past the expiration dates on the cans.

About this time our son, Jesse and his wife, Monica joined us, giving us the hope we'd be able to keep more dependable help. The added pressure of a bigger store, more merchandise and two families needing to make a living meant we needed more of the bigger orders. We couldn't survive if the building material we sold was only a few pieces at the end of the job. But a competitor held the trump card that took the business somewhere else.

An Arizona supplier was running deliveries across the state line and getting by without charging sales tax, thus giving themselves a price advantage of several hundred dollars on every truckload.

The builders who saw no reason to help us reaped rewards of gratitude when they placed these out-of-state orders, which might stretch their clients' budgets to spend less on material and more on labor. Some people showed me receipts and bids. Taking off the sales tax was bait that was leading people to pay exorbitant prices I'd have been glad to match if I'd been given a chance.

I was as dissatisfied as any other overloaded taxpayer and held no malice toward anyone who found a way to save a dollar. Still nursing wounds that had never healed from the time the Tax and Revenue Department got after me I didn't want to be the one to blow the whistle. This issue, however, affected far more than one country store. The light brown trucks from that one Arizona supplier ran daily on over two hundred miles of Western New Mexico Highways between Magdalena and Silver City.

The certified public account who handled my taxes told me this competitor was liable. The moment those truck wheels rolled across that state line they were in business in my state and obligated to pay the tax. The area was full of new subdivisions and the revenues that weren't coming were having an effect on the under-funded budgets of each school district and town in a four county area.

I discussed it with our County Commissioners and School Superintendent. They didn't want to get involved. Each had to maintain local approval or they could be voted out of their job. Any misstep on my part could hasten my downfall. Everyone who found a way to save a dollar was very protective of that right.

I had been caught when the State Tax and Revenue Department was operating on information that they received from a Gestapo that had grown around the local Village Council. The tax collectors had eyes and ears in the grocery store, the post office and the church I was attending. Revenue agents that had been bold and brutal when they caught me in the wrong were now totally unconcerned. They could care less about what happened in Catron County. Weak, ''I'll look into it," promises were all the response I could get when I called with my complaints.

We were collecting around $2,000.00 each month and sending it to Santa Fe. If the enforcement division of Tax and Revenue had exercised any vigilance they could have picked up millions of dollars they were losing due to their apathy.

Across the state line it was different. If I took a small truck and gooseneck trailer through Springerville, Arizona the route passed through an inspection station. They counted the axles on the rig and charged $65.00 for a one-day permit before I could go another forty-two miles and get a load of cement block. Our local law officers wouldn't let me play on a level field. Trucks from Arizona were making deliveries in New Mexico every day and displaying out-of-state license plates. When I mentioned it to one of our deputies, he answered, "We don't bother them." My timing was bad. Our sheriff was building a new home, and stretching his dollars like everyone else.

But I received more than my share of 'bother' from the law officers that patrolled our New Mexico Highways. My kids would come home from school with stories that "The men in uniform are our friends." None of them grew up to have to drive trucks so I hope they were able to go through life and keep that attitude.

I held that view until several bad experiences led me to believe anyone who wore a gun and a badge watched for small independent truckers and saw open cash registers. One of these men was so repugnant he doesn't deserve the courtesy of camouflaging his identity. Bernalillo County Deputy, Tom Lett, set up to watch a sign in the middle of a block that said, "Thru Truck Traffic Prohibited." The location was where the main thoroughfare, Unser, changed names for two blocks and they called it Lyons.

When I saw his flashing lights behind me I was on top of the dam for the Calabacitas Arroyo. The street is wide but at that time it was striped for two-lane traffic with no parking space along the curb. It could be considered to be a bridge where Federal trucking rules prohibit stopping. I proceeded at the dangerous speed of thirty miles an hour until there was a shoulder where I could park. He followed with flashing lights, blowing siren and called for back-up by another deputy.

The temper fit he threw would have been appropriate if he'd single handedly stopped an armed robbery or rape in progress. He wouldn't let me explain that I didn't consider my trip to be through traffic—I wasn't going to Santa Fe but was planning to spend the night at my son's home a few blocks away. The deputy wouldn't listen. He went through all the usual checks of license, registration and insurance and kept me waiting for an hour while he made radio calls trying to find serious violations that weren't there. He paid no attention to dozens of larger local trucks that rattled by.

He'd been assigned the job of watching this trap to raise revenue. Public safety couldn't have been a consideration. It was also clear he thought I'd pay the fines so I could go on my way. He handed me one ticket for getting behind the "No Truck Sign" and said, "That's fifty-four dollars." Then he handed me another for failure to yield and said "That's fifty-four dollars too."

This guy was so domineering—his temper so far out of control—I worried that he was a hazard to the public when he was on the loose with a gun and a badge. It would have been much cheaper to pay the fines than to come back but I wanted my day in court. They scheduled a hearing and postponed it a couple of times, causing me to make three more trips, but I went in the truck and pulled a load each time. My son found a route that went through a school zone and bounced over some speed bumps but avoided their "No Truck" sign.

The cop failed to appear on time for court. They dismissed several cases for that reason but kept me waiting because, "He usually makes it." I finally got my chance to tell it to the judge, their signs had effectively fenced off Albuquerque's West side for trucks that came into town from that direction. Interstate 40 had four off-ramps. The ones I'd used, Paseo Del Volcan and Unser, both led into these no truck barriers. Ninety-Eighth Street at that time stopped at a dead-end and Coors didn't have the new interchange. That route led into a suicidal situation with no signal light, making a driver fight for an opening while making a left turn against six lanes of traffic. The only safe and legal way to get to where I was going would have been to go on to the North of town and come across the Rio Grande on Alameda Street. It would have taken an extra hour.

I had a personal reason for not wanting to waste that time. I planned to check up on family by spending the night at my son, Billy's house. His wife, Lori, had recently had brain surgery and we were anxious to know the outcome. They had two small daughters, two year old Katherin and baby Rebekah, whose welfare was of more concern to me than a money-hungry cop. It was important that I get to their home before the kids bedtime but this officer refused to listen. His only concern was the $108.00 he thought he was sending to his county.

At the court hearing the cop had the audacity to say. "There is always a way." His suggestion was that I could have made a right turn on Coors to avoid the dangerous left. Then I should have turned right on Iliff and turned around in Yellow Freight's yard." That would have given me a light on Iliff to get back on Coors going north.

It is a shame Yellow Freight Company didn't have someone in that court room to hear this deputy directing public traffic to turn in their private yard.

The lady judge dismissed my case with a warning for me to not get behind any more no-truck signs. She knew a new interchange was planned for Coors at I-40 and told me to be patient.

Albuquerque and Rio Rancho played musical chairs with their no-truck signs. They put them up, took them down and moved them around. There was no way to predict when I'd make a turn and find one had appeared in the middle of some block with no way to avoid violating it. This incident and others which soon followed gave me a permanent distrust of any officer parked beside the road watching traffic.

My weekly 450 mile circle through either of two routes from my home to Albuquerque and back led me through five counties, several villages, and two Indian Reservations. They all had their police, marshals, or deputies.

There were also the State Police and the Motor Transportation Department which targeted only the heavy truckers. They all had cars on the road with red lights and they all were looking for money. The towns of Magdalena and Socorro put their speed limit signs a couple of miles out of town. I never got caught in their traps but usually saw someone who had. Many times I've sat there and let my foot get too heavy while driving through open range. My time will probably come.

I tried to be a law abiding driver with late-model rigs in good repair, but drew more than my share of traffic stops. All of them were trivial and once an officer got a rig stopped he usually found some reason to write several warnings or citations. A crack in a windshield or a smear of dripping oil was all they needed.

One Transportation Department officer pulled me over for no D.O.T. number painted on my door. I'd filled out the paperwork, sent it to Santa Fe and nothing came back. He found more violations, Improper Registration for a trailer and Expired Safety Inspection though his outfit had put that sticker on the truck windshield.

This man was reasonably courteous and gave me a phone number to find out what had happened to my D.O.T. application. I'd previously been stopped at one of their portable scale inspections and they had wasted an hour while they went over the rig with white gloves. They'd given me a fifteen day warning to get a brake adjusted which was also a piece of paper to sign and send to Santa Fe. There was no extra copy for myself and I didn't have the foresight to make one. I had kept no paper-work to prove the date. This was probably meant as a lesson for me to go to the shops that sold inspection stickers and keep them current.

The improper registration citation was the most ridiculous. The worst display of temper the officer had given was when he found the code U.T. on my paperwork and stormed, "That's not a utility trailer. It should be F.T. for freight trailer."

"Hell, I don't know. I went to the license office and wrote a check. I put on whatever they gave me."

At home I checked my title and found the trailer had been coded F.T. when I bought it. So I went to the girl that sold license plates and bawled her out for changing the code and getting me in trouble.

Her answer was, "That cop doesn't know what he's talking about. The Motor Vehicle Department has combined those classifications. They are the same."

Before we got cell phone service another cop who showed no understanding and no willingness to listen was a Laguna Tribal Policeman at the Dancing Eagle Casino. While waiting for our next grandson to arrive, we had been keeping our two-year old granddaughter, Mattie, who was asleep, strapped to a child's seat and wet in the truck cab. I needed to stop at a pay phone to tell my son when to meet us in Albuquerque. In front of the casino convenience store there is a wide shoulder where I could keep the truck in view while I made the call. I'd hardly got it stopped when the cop appeared and commanded, "You can't park here! Trucks park in the rear! You're blocking the view."

I wasn't going to leave that baby alone among several acres of parked trucks and it was going to be an ugly scene if I woke her up and tried to keep her with me, crying, while I made the call. I tried explaining, "I just need to make a quick phone call…"

He wouldn't let me finish.

"I said get it out of here." There wasn't no signs posted to prohibit parking. This guy made his own laws to suit his personal desires.

124

I got out of that one by pulling into a fuel lane and making their paying customers wait while I was on the phone. There I could call while keeping the truck in view.

The New Mexico State Police used Catron County for a training ground for rookies. Young, by the book and knowing all the rules we quickly learned they'd get us if they could. That happened to me one night when Patrolman Shawn Healey pulled me over for the unforgivable sin of no light on my license plate. Some bump in the road or bush in a pasture had given me a hole in the bumper where the bulb was supposed to be. Then he searched my vehicle and found an old dirty smashed beer can. He shook it, got a couple drops and claimed 15% was remaining. He wrote two citations—one for the missing light and another for an open container—though he penciled a note that there was no smell of alcohol on my breath. He made them out to require court appearances.

I found my opening when I read his vehicle description. He'd described white paint as silver on both tickets.

I carried the papers to Magistrate Judge Clayton Atwood, a friendly young man I'd known since he was born, telling him, "When this gets to court I'm going to testify this cop isn't competent to give a description of a vehicle after he stops it."

In a few days Atwood was in my store and told me, "You don't have to appear in court. The cop dismissed your charges."

Conflicting rules cause confusion. No truck carries a light for a license plate on the front bumper but a Motor Transportation officer got upset and threatened a citation, claiming my registration at the rear of the truck wasn't visible. It was blocked from his view under the trailer. But the instructions on each annual renewal say 'Place on rear of vehicle.'

The only consolation I could find for the hours of time they wasted was they appeared busy, made a show of doing something to earn their pay, making me wait and watch other traffic slow as they went around those flashing lights.

This should not be interpreted as an indictment or criticism of all law officers. There was a morning at the small convenience store at

Quemado Lake when I was serving on a volunteer search and rescue team. We had spent an afternoon and then a night in near-zero temperatures looking for a disoriented elk hunter who hadn't returned to camp. Our stomachs and fuel gauges were running on empty. We found gasoline but it looked like their best choice for breakfast was going to be cold drinks and candy bars.

State Policeman Larry Blount insisted we come to his nearby mobile home. Quietly, with the rest of his family still asleep, he fried all the eggs and toasted the last slice of their bread but sent us on our way with a hot breakfast under our belts.

At another time Thelma was released from a hospital in Albuquerque following some medial tests and she needed a ride home. I had made promises to deliver building material that day and it would mess up someone's job schedule if I went elsewhere. State Policeman Mike Shriver went beyond the call of duty by making the trip on his own time, driving my car to bring her back.

We had a number of good, friendly helpful law officers. I had multiple dealings with Shriver and Shawn Menges and never a hint of any problems. Our County Deputy Jimmy Jaramillo and State Police Officer Steve Owens both pulled me over at times I was in the wrong and made warnings out of what could have been legitimate citations. In both cases I can compliment them and say they were doing their jobs. I tell of all those bad experiences because I think these other officer's salaries could have bought more public benefit if they'd aimed their belligerent attitudes in a more productive direction. They should have been fighting real crime without having to extort their subsistence from people who had to use the public roads for a place to make a living.

It was disgusting to watch the news and see how many bureaucrats were getting their fingers in the taxpayer's pocket on some pretense of assisting economic development, but I was trying to make a living for my family and provide a necessary service for my community and faced an uphill battle at every turn. The Tax and Revenue Department and the Construction Industries Commission had worked with the Town Government to run me out of town. Then when an out-of-state competitor had me locked in a stranglehold that made it impossible for my prices to be competitive there was no one from any agency who would go to bat in my defense.

126

I had to dodge cops every trip to haul home the things I had to sell to keep the business going.

Chapter Fourteen

BOB

I could do nothing that suited Bob. He was always complaining. My store, my methods of operation, my prices and the quality of the merchandise were his favorite topics of conversation. He appointed himself to the position of town watchdog and thought he should be honored for the service he provided. Then he waded into that task with an attitude that was only suitable for the Captain of God's team. Some locals nicknamed him "God." They designated other men named Robert as "Big Belly Bob," "Grouchy Bob" or "Nervous Bob." It just fell into place to call this one "Bitchin' Bob."

There were several other Bobs who were friendly, honest and helpful. The only accurate way to mention them is by using both first and last name. None of them play a part in this narrative.

Bob wanted everyone to know he was a perfectionist. He mixed this message into every word he spoke, every breath he took and every move he made, trying to project his goals of complete and total quality in everything he did. He wanted to use only the best tools and material and spent all his waking hours chanting a monologue about the excellent quality of his work. He fully exercised his right to free speech, telling everyone he was the only man who had ever come to this town who could deliver all the first class advantages.

He gave himself the right to denounce anyone or anything that didn't measure up to his ideals. I earned his full time criticism. He was never silent. Any store worthy of his patronage should stock everything he needed and sell it for a price he approved. If we didn't have the exact thing he asked for, he let loose a fist-pounding, foot stomping, "They make it!" If he wanted something that wasn't in the catalog it was "You should find a reliable supplier!"

There was a mutual contempt between Bob and my dog, a contest in which the dog usually got kicked but he considered it to be his duty to mark everyone's tires. I overlooked it as something that happened wherever there were dogs to check automobile tires.

Bob never came through the door without letting us know he judged a store by their price tags, "They're making something!" was his reason to explain why a small store set up to serve a little country town should match the prices of the big box retailers. The perfect builder should only shop at the perfect store so he made it clear he'd always pass us by if he could find a way to fill his needs elsewhere, even though we failed miserably in all his evaluations, prices that were a rip-off, a selection that was a disgrace and service he called totally unacceptable. He expounded on the notion he should be given the authority to open charge accounts for anyone who hired him. Because he was scrupulous and conscientious the people he worked for should be also.

Bob had several carefully memorized spiels to give his listeners his opinion on any subject. Sports, politics, religion or physical fitness were all topics he could discuss at length and then route the conversation back to the perfect qualities of his work and the sorry state of affairs when a town had nothing better than my store for a supplier. Never bashful or shy, he forced us to listen to his abusive tirades whether he was at our counter or in the next booth at a café.

He assumed squatter's rights to a vacant lot on Main Street. From that observation point he could watch to see who entered each of the cafes, the bar and whoever might occupy the loafer's bench in front of the convenience store. Anyone who paused a few moments at one of those gathering places was assured of him coming to give his lecture.

Reports came that his enthusiasm for condemning us was fueled by a sales commission he was drawing from our principal competitor. He was especially proud that he could get orders from out of state and avoid any sales tax.

His specialty was masonry which gave him the opportunity to start everyone's job. He turned out work that was meticulous in detail. Straight lines, level and square with exact measurements—there was no way to find fault with the quality of his craftsmanship. He talked and labored without stopping. When the foundation was finished most of his clients were convinced they should avoid my store as if it were infected with plague.

Some customers believed him, some ignored him, and others came to tell us what he was doing to us. Their reports were no surprise.

He worked for me on at least three occasions and his ranting and raving continued even while I was writing his paycheck. He often added emphasis to his statements by saying, "In my expert opinion."

On one occasion he threw a fit about the price of some piece of merchandise and yelled, "It doesn't cost that much to go to Albuquerque!"

I walked to my desk and picked up an unpaid bill for $3,000.00 in insurance, made him a copy and told him, "That's part of my cost of doing business. It comes twice a year. Figure it out yourself. It's over $115.00 a week and I can't operate without it."

He threw the paper in the floor without looking and stomped out the door saying. "That's yours!" He continued to stand beside Main Street and tell everyone I was robbing them without any acknowledgement that I had to pay my bills.

Fully aware of his open and continuous hostility I continued to send material to his jobs because I appreciated the quality of his work and recognized his contribution to the town. He could speak Spanish which made him all the more useful to some of the oldest and least affluent members of the community. But they let me know he was adept at condemning me in both languages.

When we had to be gone a few days I inserted some humor into the argument with a sign on our driveway gate. "Check the deals at Bob's store" it told most observers he was whipping a dead horse. There was nothing to be gained from criticizing and condemning a business that wasn't open.

It started a turn-around in local attitude. We'd tolerated enough and we weren't going to stay to take this abuse forever.

Our final collision with Bob came over a dispute over the price of a sack of roofing screws. All three of my roofing suppliers sold screws that attached their product to wood framing with a quarter-inch hexagon head. If the frame was made of metal purlins the screw head was five-sixteenths. A little short stitch screw was sometimes used for edge laps. It took the five-sixteenths socket wrench. Bob spent years complaining it was too much trouble to have to change socket sizes in his drill. He gave me the "They make it!" argument. None of my suppliers could help him.

Persistence finally paid off and I got a phone number of a supplier who sold the screws he wanted. But instead of the regular next week delivery that package would come by parcel delivery—several days slower. Now his complaints were "I need it all at once! You are going to make me go back to the job for a few screws. Then he ordered a bag of the special screws in a color that wasn't stocked by this new supplier. They tacked on a $20.00 service charge for custom painting. This combined with the added shipping cost meant I had to charge him almost $50.00 for a bag of screws that would have normally sold under $20.00. He refused to accept them. "Send 'em back! I don't want 'em!"

It was a special order I couldn't return. I tossed them in the trash and told him, "Get out of here!"

That caused gossip to roll through the town. Most of the people heard the news from Bob and took his side of the argument. Now he had to send other people to my store to do his shopping.

He started to feel the pain when he needed something in too big a hurry to get it from out of town.

Several months passed. Too late, he must have realized it was worth something to have access to his needs in a local store. Now he put a big smile on his face and spoke a friendly greeting when we met on the street. He'd wave if he recognized my vehicle approaching on the road.

On a cold, cloudy, totally miserable afternoon near the little town of Buckhorn I stopped for a hitchhiker. A half-frozen man was holding one hand in the air, trying to thumb a ride. His other arm was also raised, holding onto a broad-brimmed straw hat to keep it from blowing away. Sunset was coming fast. I couldn't pass such a pathetic-looking sight. Now Bob had an hour and a half to sit in the back seat of my car and try to make conversation without saying bad things about me. I remained silent and let him stammer. This situation had come up as a result of him riding to Silver City with his girlfriend. Something caused her to go somewhere else and leave him to hitchhike home.

Twenty –four years had passed since he moved here. I had run my business three years longer which meant he's spent nearly as much time trying to tear it apart as I'd spent building it.

Afterwards he smiled and offered a handshake every time we met. I appreciated his change in attitude and tried to go forward without malice. By now our stock had dwindled so much there was little for anyone to come back for.

He'd never realized we were pushing forward thinking our most profitable business tactic was to have the item a customer needed when he asked for it. It was a situation where what we spent bought us nothing. There was no way for us to gain from what we bought and stored. Someone had to buy it at a price we could replace it and keep something for ourselves for profit, or we were working for nothing. So the health of the business was measured by speed of turnover, not by the person who watched Main Street and voiced his complaints to everyone he could stop.

Chapter Fifteen

GETTING OUT

Our plans of building a store that would serve the community into the next generation crashed and burned in a moment when our son, Jesse, went home and found a note: "Dear Jesse, I'm sorry it had to end this way, but I don't love you any more. I want a divorce. Monica." She was gone and she'd taken our grandson, Michael, with her. She closed all the doors to communication and refused to consider any reconciliation. I got the blame as being hard too work for, but most of the evidence points toward her wanting to get back closer to her mother.

Before the shock wore off, we knew the only way for Jesse to retain any control or be any part of Michael's life would be for him to live and work close to wherever she took him.

He'd modernized our business when he tied all the bookkeeping into the computer. Thelma was learning the basics but I refused to have anything to do with it. Jesse stayed a while giving her some crash courses then they burned a lot of midnight oil on the phone as she learned each step one at a time.

I started looking for ways to get out. The business had grown to be more than Thelma and I could handle alone and we'd had very poor luck keeping dependable help. The town was becoming dependent on us but most of them thought it was necessary to appear dissatisfied with everything we did. It looked like the best thing for everyone concerned would be for us to sell out to someone who could give them what they wanted.

A growing business in a place that had no competition and in a trade area that was expanding should have been attractive to a lot of buyers. I'd been spending $1,500.00 to $2,000.00 a year on new barn space. Our insurance salesman had watched it grow, counted square feet and added $10,000.00 to $20,000.00 a year to the replacement coverage. Our net worth was increasing. Continual expansion meant money never stayed in our hands but the turnover increased each year.

The added inventory gave us some violent shocks at tax time but we thought that was one of the costs of building a successful business.

The most convenient arrangement for us or a potential buyer would require blocking off about twenty acres which would include our home and a rent house. Survey lines were in place which would include three high-demand building sites along the top of a bluff with a beautiful view overlooking the San Francisco river valley. They could have been subdivided and sold for enough to leave the business free of debt.

We made plans to move to a spot beyond the next hill, keep on running a little bunch of cattle, and build a new home for a place to retire.

The coffee shop crowd was overjoyed. Again we heard, "If you'll get out of the way the next owner might give us a real store." We stayed with the business another ten years without finding a serious buyer or real estate broker who gave a damn about net worth. They looked for profit and return on investment. Community needs and service counted nothing.

Our chickens were coming home to roost. We'd voluntarily helped a lot of people while another bunch forced us to give them more help than we wanted. We had to open our books and our tax records for potential buyers. Every slow-paying customer, every act of shoplifting, and everyone who had gone somewhere else to buy had their effect as these people analyzed our business history. In order to present our business to a buyer we needed a local acceptance and a profit picture we'd never enjoyed.

We'd never found a way to get enough of our clients to give us a chance to bid on their major orders. Those who did were usually satisfied that we saved them enough trouble to justify any additional price. We couldn't overcome two misconceptions, better deals always came from bigger stores and the lowest price is the best deal. This led people to go two hundred miles for metal roofing, manufactured in Lubbock, Texas and hauled to Albuquerque stores on the same day of the week, the same truck, and at about the same price as we got it delivered to our yard. My low mark-up and free delivery gave us a price advantage they wouldn't bother to investigate.

136

Our customers had never learned we didn't have that magic lamp we should be able to rub so anything they wanted would fall out of the sky. Those we'd managed to satisfy had never been as vocal as those who couldn't be pleased. Some potential buyers complained because our place couldn't be seen from a main road. It had evolved a little at a time while we had done the best we could with what we had. A highly visible business location had never been available and there had never been money in our budget to buy land. We didn't want to sell our home and hated to sell any part of the ranch but we would have done so to keep the business going. We priced the whole package and offered to trim it to fit if anyone came our way who was interested.

Several real-estate brokers came and went. Some for a six month listing, others worked as much as two years. They found several lookers but no takers. Some buyers would have jumped at a chance to get the acreage but they didn't want to be saddled with the business. There was no guarantee the next person would be interested in selling lumber or hardware. We listened to plans to convert the buildings to apartments or the inventory to feed and western clothes.

We forged ahead, trying to make the annual turnover grow. Anything we could do to increase the volume should make it more attractive to a buyer. We welcomed any chance to give a customer some help with planning or a delivery. That led us into filling some absurd requests. The persistent ringing of a phone interrupted the opening prayer one Sunday in church. Someone went to the next room to answer it, then passed the word to me that it was my call. A well-known and respected member of the community was serious but impatient when he told me, "I need a light bulb. Bring your ladder with you when you deliver it so you can put it in for me."

We never promised round-the-clock service, but a contractor that was so undependable in making his payments we'd had to prosecute him in court, had the audacity to ask us to start opening at 6:00 a.m. in case his crew needed something before they went to work.

Customers kept Thelma busy all day answering "How much is it?" questions and telling her they could get a better price somewhere else. She stayed up half the night caring for the books, ordering, pricing; tax reports and payroll were endless jobs because everything had to be done on time. I was usually sound asleep before her day's work was done. One night she had barely got into bed when a desperate lady called, "I need paint thinner! I borrowed a paint sprayer and it will ruin if I don't clean it!"

"Why didn't you get it before you started?" Thelma was so mad she woke me up.

"I didn't need it then." The lady lived a half-hour away so Thelma lost another hour of sleep.

It was tempting to disconnect the phone but we stayed ready for the times we could help them out of their real emergencies. We helped the people when pipes broke, roofs blew off or something knocked out a window. However I didn't consider it to be an emergency one night when a blowing horn and flashing headlights brought me out of bed around midnight. This lady wanted a paint roller. Since she had me awake I took care of her, taking a $1.35 check which bounced, but she said, "I'm sure glad you stayed open for me." Then she got mad when I called her to tell about her check, telling me, "If that's the way you're going to treat me I'll never go back to that place."

After a time a really interested buyer looked at our business. It looked as if he was what we were waiting for. His desire was to tear up some roots in the Midwest, move here, and sell hardware. He had some cash available for a down payment. But he was cautious and he wasn't going take the plunge until he thought everything was right.

He spent days looking at the books, the stock and the care that had gone into the construction of the buildings. He ran through computer programs to work out a payment schedule and made me adjust the price down until he thought he saw a comfortable margin of safety.

Then one day he went to town for lunch. There were three cafes operating at the time and I had bad debt cases pending in court against two of them. All of them had a malicious bunch of loafers drinking coffee and giving advice on how everyone should run their business.

Our buyer came back saying, "I'm sorry. I've got to think about this. You've sure done a poor job of getting this town to accept you! I don't want to spend my life's savings to be the most despised person in town." Months later he bought a store in another town.

In that café someone had unleashed an abrasive tirade about our business practices. Someone wanted to stop a dripping faucet. They didn't want to spend .59 cents on a package of assorted rubber washers. We should stock them in bulk, install them, and cure their problem for a dime. Our own experience with bulk parts was that people would mix the various sizes together, throw the beveled ones into the compartment for the flat, scatter them all over the floor, put their used washers in with our new stock and leave the store complaining about poor service but carrying away our screwdriver concealed in their pocket.

Someone had moved to center stage when he found the opportunity to entertain everyone within ear shot with his caustic sarcasm. He scared off our buyer and killed the best chance that ever came along to pass the business on to someone who wanted to keep it alive, all over a half-dollar complaint.

The designation "most despised in town" was a fitting finale to our years of trying to provide services to the community. We had helped people every day and most had left satisfied but there had always been some who were discontented. Those who were upset were vocal and made sure everyone knew their objections. Any coffee shop is full of the type. They are not working and aren't trying to be an asset to their community.

Now this loudmouth made his permanent contribution to the local area. When we closed our doors there were no faucet washers, in any size of package for anyone to complain. Everyone had to spend a half-day on the road to check out the next store.

When we'd used up all the dependable local real estate brokers without finding a buyer we tried some business brokers. This little place out in the country enraged them. One came to look at it but couldn't wait to leave. Another studied our books then wouldn't return a phone call. Little Mom and Pop businesses that closed because they couldn't compete with the big ones were common. Then we tried others who required us to put up their advertising money in advance. They claimed their lists of buyers covered a world-wide market and used the "You have to spend money to make money" approach. They compiled personalized books full of charts and graphs from our profit and loss statements and income tax records.

The first ones baited their hooks with a claim they would refund our money if they couldn't find us a buyer. I paid them $8,000.00 and only got one name and address for my money. Now I realized they could have found names in phone books or on tombstones. That one hint of a response kept them from any obligation for the refund.

Passing retirement age and watching the strain take its toll on Thelma I tried another business broker. This one cost us $7,000.00 and they claimed to have a higher success rate than the first. They must have been more diligent about copying tombstones because we received the contact information for several possible buyers. We gave all of them personal follow up letters and phone calls.

That brought me into a conversation with one irate buyer who had taken a close look at our financial information. "There's something fishy about these figures," he charged. "You don't show enough gross receipts to support the growth in net worth. Where did you get the money to add these barns and trucks and inventory?"

"I built this business as money came in from a ranch I'd sold." I told him.

"I thought so! It's a fraud! You ought to be in jail." He hung up.

I thought I was presenting a picture of what was here rather than where it came from, but I couldn't prevent someone's reading between the lines to find information I hadn't offered.

A windbag walked through the door to tell me he was going to start an add-on but, "You're not going to rob me with your prices. I've got my own truck and I'll haul it."

"Let me bid on it." I told him.

He drove a light-duty pickup with four-ply tires and hauled a tool box that would shift the weight of a load to the rear.

He had a rough idea of how many feet long by how many wide, no concept of what he'd have to buy to build it.

This was common. I'd spend hours helping him make a plan before either of us knew what he needed. We had to discuss all the alternatives like whether to use lumber framing or concrete for the floor. Would the roof be shingles or metal?

His answer to those questions was, "What's cheapest?"

I priced out several alternate plans, which he carried to competitors to bid against me.

He was back in a few days, rude as ever, with "I told you so! Your price is the highest on everything on the list."

I always welcomed the chance to compare prices, especially when a written quote gave me something I could see for myself regarding what I was up against. This competitor hadn't helped him with a plan and only given him the price per cement block and the price per square of shingles etc. I had to go through the list again to find where I stood at the bottom line. I also ran a total on the weight of the order.

He moved nearly five thousand pounds, which took several trips, to save seventy-five dollars on an order I'd have charged nothing extra to deliver to his job.

It was a daily scene in our business life. We were caught between trying to please buyers who wanted to see us make more profit and customers who wouldn't pay what we thought we needed to survive. Although we needed every sale we could get I found myself with less and less patience with the people who gave us a bad time every time they came.

One old fellow concluded every visit with a routine that included going through each pocket, while crying that we were "Taking from the poor to give to the rich." He always took several minutes, holding up traffic at the check-out stand, while he fished a few coins out of each pocket. A day came that he wanted a horseshoe—less than a two-dollar purchase—and he wanted everyone to wait while he went out to his car to look for more money.

I lost my composure, took the horseshoe back, and told him to go somewhere else to get it.

Several months passed. He had a large family of cousins and nephews who all boycotted our store. Then a night came when Thelma and I were eating in a local café. The waitress came around to tell us, "That man over there paid for your meal." He was sitting quietly in a far back corner.

I went over and thanked him. He had tears in his eyes when he said, "You can't take a joke."

What else would we have to tolerate to serve these people?

The money that was coming from the sale of the ranch dried up. The good man who now owned it hadn't been able make the payments with what came from the cattle so he risked his life with a civilian job in the Iraq war. He accomplished his goal of paying his way out of debt. We lost a big chunk of his money when we paid our income tax and no longer had that cushion of outside money coming when people were slow about paying us.

As the word got out that we were going to quit people started to realize what shopping out of town for all of their small orders was going to cost them. One man came in who had taken the lead building a large church complex. They had spent years making lots of small purchases without checking to see if we could be competitive on their larger orders. The tax-free bait from the out of state competitor was probably their reason. He nearly cried when he said, It's sure going to be expensive to go get everything now."

The listings expired with the brokers who were going to sell our business. We weren't getting any younger. We had to choose between liquidating the stock and dieing in the harness because it looked like we'd committed ourselves to a life sentence. We spent another year trying to downsize by restocking only the most necessary items.

Lack of help increased the urgency. Two good men left our team because they could make more money at other jobs. I couldn't blame them. One good dependable lady, Helen Milligan, worked for us eleven years. She'd retired from another job, but at age seventy-eight she had to admit it was time to stop.

142

I quit handling lumber, an item that had bought me nothing but mad customers. We dropped the Ben Franklin line of merchandise. The town had stormed into our store to get cheap toilet paper but every month's sale found us looking at piles of leftover Halloween costumes or chocolate Easter Bunnies, worthless after that holiday passed. Now we could see it was a mistake for us to pay help to handle merchandise that wasn't making a profit. Each month's sales brought us grumbling and moaning and more mad customers when we wouldn't let those items we were handling below cost go out on credit.

I sold my trucks. But I'd developed a habit of watching every cop parked beside the road and expecting his lights to come up in my rear view mirror. Now it is hard to remember I'm driving something too small to matter when I find those "No Truck" signs that Albuquerque shuffles from the middle of one block to the next.

We locked the door and took a trip to Yellowstone. This gave us two weeks that we didn't have to run to the phone to answer someone's "How much is it?" We began to see there were pleasures in life that didn't come from trying to help people. We could put our money into our own pleasures instead of items for people to fondle or steal.

My downfall will probably be tied to my answering the advertisements that came in bulk-rate mail. Several companies offered to assist with sales to close stores. I selected one that kept coming from the G. A. Wright Company. Their lead information looked good, making us think they would help us empty the store "to the bare walls" while recovering about ten percent more than our cost if we let them run a five and a half week sale. Their fees were going to be expensive but promised a better return than we could expect from an auction or anything we could do ourselves. They told us to quit worrying about the computer and the barcodes. We wouldn't need them anymore.

Their mass advertising ahead of the sale created a mob scene. Parked cars filled all our space and both shoulders of our half-mile driveway. There wasn't elbow room to walk through the store. All those people came looking for bargains. There had never been so many pockets that could be filled or so many fingers messing with the merchandise.

If it is cheap enough someone may take it, but we stood no chance of recovering our cost at the prices they wanted to mark. I let the representative sacrifice some items for leaders and go down to my cost on others. For the most part I gambled someone might need it sometime.

The big crowd was gone in a few hours. The G. A. Wright plan was to get everyone to sign in for chances to win a color T. V., power tools, and other valuable prizes. That gave us a mailing list to invite them back for further price reductions—more money out of my pocket at every step.

We moved a lot of merchandise but the sale ended with thousands of dollars tied up in what was still on the shelves. Their representative had moved it to strange locations and re-priced it with permanent ink. Their refusal to use the computer meant we had no way to know how many pieces we owned of any item. We had to close the door for two months to re-do the inventory. We enjoyed a new-found freedom. Now we gave ourselves the pleasure of two weeks in Alaska. Then we came back to a building still half-full of merchandise someone had at sometime demanded we carry in our stock. Some of the town was glad to find our doors open again. They quickly picked off the most common items. It became embarrassing to try to fill most orders. If we had the right bolt there was no nut to fit it. They'd buy a gallon of paint and we had no brushes or rollers. Any thought of restocking a few basics was leading us back into the mess we were trying to get out of.

My tactic of stocking leftovers to build inventory sometimes jumped up to bite me. A friendly and helpful customer ordered fifty sheets of three-quarter inch tongue and grooved plywood. Everyone else used a cheaper product made of chips and glue called O.S.B. I had to buy in bundle quantity, which came to ninety-two pieces, then hope someone would want the remaining forty-two. When his job was done he returned six sheets, saying, "I wanted to make sure you got me plenty. Now I had forty-eight pieces of a high priced product no one else wanted.

Many people thought we were completely out of business and quit coming. We saw a picture of a future in which we couldn't live long enough to recover all our investment.

144

There are countless factual stories about people who started with nothing, spent their lives at hard work, with honest dealings and frugal management, and went on to build successful businesses. The key to their prosperity always hinged on the fact they provided a product or service someone needed. I'm not aware of anyone who ever reached the top while half of his clients were working against him. Ours was a success story up to the point where we tried to get someone to step into our shoes and keep it going. When it was time for someone else to carry the ball, there was no one who was willing to do the work or take the risk.

Now the friendly people who had come to depend on us were the ones who were upset. They thought we were deserting them.

These communities, Reserve, Aragon and Luna had been built along the sides of mountain streams and irrigation ditches in the 1880's. No one had to walk more than a quarter-mile to fill his bucket with water. Within a few years most of the people had access to a hand-dug well where they could pull the bucket out of the ground with a rope. Then pumps, pipes and indoor plumbing changed all that to where all they had to do was turn the handle of a faucet. Many no longer owned a bucket. Now for the past twenty-seven years they had counted on us to be able to fix almost anything that stopped the flow of the water.

We sympathized with them. The same problems would hit us too. But every cowboy is familiar with the adage, "You can lead a horse to water but you can't make him drink." I'd have to quote that proverb to anyone who might ever tell me he was thinking of starting a store in any small town. It is what Eddie Peter was trying to tell me when he cautioned, "If your town gets behind you."

EPILOGUE

The events described in these two chapters happened after we'd tried to retire, sold most of the ranch and closed our hardware store. I tolerated my cousin's indifference, fixed his fences and cared for his stock for over fifty years without making any public complaint but when he cut the chain, took the lock and endangered my property he gave me reason to leave this account.

The enemies I made when I tried to keep a small struggling church from closing its door also fit in with the same theme, adding another chapter. Trouble should quit looking for me when they bury me. Between now and then I'll probably keep making people mad when I try to help them.

Chapter Sixteen

NEIGHBORS BY SPITE

A desire to be a good neighbor has been the driving force behind most of the things I've done. I tried to assist quietly, with no bells or whistles and no trumpets blaring, better yet if they didn't know what I'd done. In the ranch life that meant I tried to maintain more than half of each boundary fence. But that never meant I wanted to do it all alone. Likewise I considered that the ownership of a ranch carried the moral obligation to work with each neighbor keeping the fences repaired. Those ethics weren't always shared by the persons on the other side of the fence.

My uncle made it part of his religion to ride around and check all of each fence every year. He thought I should do the same and didn't hesitate to give me a strong reprimand if I fell short on my responsibility. While hard-working and fair, he was also very possessive and quick to anger if any neighbor's cow crossed a fence and ate his grass. He'd owned his ranch so long while keeping it debt free, he had no appreciation for the fact younger operators had to prop up their operations with money from a non-agricultural source.

I maintained a hectic pace keeping jobs going to make a living, handling the day-to-day needs of a ranch, a growing family and maintaining without help, some sixty-five miles of fences.

I incorrectly assumed the ethics of one generation would be passed to the next. My uncle and my cousin, Glen, both used my corrals for shipping and branding their cattle. When maintenance work was needed my uncle would join me, even if it was for a day of digging postholes. When he noticed I'd replaced a rotten gate he voluntarily handed me the money I'd spent on lumber. As soon as my cousin took over the management of that ranch he sent a hired hand who didn't know how to back a stock-trailer; he knocked two gate posts out of the ground and left the mess for me to fix.

My uncle did all he could until he was in his eighties. He gave his son part of his ranch and cattle to get some help with his work. But my cousin made his living from coin-operated machines. He started small, reinvested and built up routes that kept several people busy servicing juke boxes, vending machines and amusement devices such as pinball machines and coin-operated pool tables. His business was successful; the profits rolled in and he managed to buy several ranches. Ownership of ranch property was a tool wealthy people used to save on income tax. Their accountants could play with range improvements, depreciation schedules and capital gains deductions, lose money, and still come out ahead of where they would have been if they'd paid their tax without it.

His frequent statement, "I ain't got time," seemed to absolve him of any responsibility to work on the fences and his frugal penny pinching nature kept him from hiring help to assist his neighbors.

He bought one ranch from me and tried to stretch minimal payments beyond the end of a twenty-year contract. All the while he was buying more ranches, clearly showing he was assembling an empire he didn't try to keep in any reasonable state of repair. His coin machine routes kept him gone from home a lot and his stock drifted where they pleased. When other neighbors or the sheriff's department couldn't reach him they called me. Sometimes it was his wife who called me for assistance when situations arose she couldn't handle. I found myself herding his cattle by moonlight to get them off the highway.

Never uttering a word of thanks, he let me know he didn't appreciate my meddling when our elderly widowed neighbor, Enid McCargish, asked me to help get a bunch of his cattle out of her yard and garden. The hole in their fence had been part of his scheme to take over her place.

My uncle tried to do the fence riding for these new ranches. He stayed with it until he was frail, senile and weak, presenting a pathetic picture as he'd try to prop up a rotten post with a stick the size of a broom handle. When he was completely worn out, his son hired a man out of Mexico and gave him more work than triplets could have handled. Fence work was hurriedly done when it was not absolutely necessary that he be working cattle.

My ranch joined theirs for some twenty miles, including five water-gaps in stream bottoms where everything washed away in each major storm. I fixed them all alone time after time because I didn't

150

want to add to my uncle's load. It became obvious they had decided I was such a good neighbor they'd never have to worry about any fence that joined my place. While I had no problem with his priorities, we were both aware of the source of our finances. I needed to do my part on the ranch then get back to my unfinished construction problems.

A series of monster floods destroyed several quarter-mile strips. New wire and steel posts had to be brought in six miles by pack horse. This was too big a contribution to donate without recognition or assistance. This cousin had a teen aged son who, if he ever got interested, could have been a lot of help. Seldom involved in the ranch work, he spent a lot of time riding around on one of those early model three-wheel ATV machines. He came along one day when I was fixing one of those flood-damaged fences, sat on the stream bank and visited while I worked alone. When my uncle thanked me for getting the job done, I complained. "You know Ricky was there the whole time and never helped a bit.

My uncle's answer was, "I couldn't even get Glen to go to the job at that age. If I took him he'd cry he wanted to go back home."

One of his ranches was in Arizona and reported to summer some 400 head of cattle. There were times when he moved them home, he gave no warning, checked no fence, and jumped them out of the trucks on Higgins Flat about two miles north of my home. They headed south, downhill along an old worn-out fence. The next waterhole was a pond in my front yard. I came home from one building job and found Thelma and our three small children in a frenzy chasing cattle out of her garden.

I had to do something. He'd gone too far on this free ride. The Forest Service furnished new barbed wire and steel posts to rebuild the fence except where the job entered private land.

I called him to see if he would split the cost of the labor. His response was "Yes. After the cattle are shipped this fall you can have my hired hand." But he kept finding things he considered more urgent than the fence job for the man to do.

Never very friendly, now I could observe open hostility in his body language anytime we met.

Some of my cattle weren't accounted for so I checked Ramon Trujillo's Cox Canyon allotment. At the Dutchman Tank I found one little heifer of mine with sixteen of Glen's. The fence was bad. There were open gates at both the top and bottom ends of the water lot, several elk breaks and a long stretch was on the ground where rotten posts had fallen.

There were too many cattle to handle alone. There was about an hour of remaining daylight. Clouds were moving in and we'd had a forecast of snow for that eight thousand foot elevation. I had to keep them at that tank overnight and hope I could get help to bring them out the next day.

I rode circles around the tank and tried to keep them quiet. I'd step off and quickly close a gate, prop up a fallen post, or make some other hasty repair. A couple of cows were at each end of the bunch wanting to leave and ready to try their move any time I wasn't in front of them. There were loose scraps of wire I could use for patches. By dark I had something standing that resembled a fence. A call to Glen aggravated him because I was interrupting his plans for the next day. But he sent Joe Peterson, his son-in-law at the time, with another horse and trailer—acting like he was doing me a favor by helping. We got only an inch of snow, chilling when it fell off limbs. This was enough to make the cattle feisty but my makeshift fence had held. The nearest place to load a trailer was on the other side of the mountain at Skip Price's Five Springs Tank. Joe and I got both trailers loaded and brought them home without incident. Glen was waiting at his corral to look them over.

By now I'd spent two days and burned two tanks of gas to return one little heifer that had mixed with his bunch when they crossed the fence. Good neighbors never charged each other for helping but the friendly ones watched for situations like this and replaced fuel that was consumed. Not Glen—he frowned, looked the other way and said, "Now we can get back to our work!" Again I'd upset his scheme to use someone else's grass.

He remained surly and uncommunicative until December when my son, Jesse, was home from college on Christmas break. There was also a young man in jail for assaulting a deputy sheriff. They would let him out if he could find a job. I always made use of help when I could find it. We built the fence and by working on each foot of it myself, it came out being a much higher quality job than if I'd used all hired labor.

My cousin ignored the bill I sent him. When I threatened court action he sent a letter refusing payment because half of the responsibility was mine and claimed I'd used the wrong hired hand for his part.

It was traumatic; my first bad debt case and I was plaintiff against a cousin. But I wasn't going to give away that much money or labor without a fight. I learned I should know if the defendant owned the judge before I filed a case. The magistrate was schooled as a lawyer but he was spending most of his time working on his own ranch. He listened to our arguments, including Glen's ridiculous claim that two or three days should have been enough to rebuild two miles of fence. After deciding the case in my favor he awarded me $250.00 on a $2,000.00 debt. A few days later I understood his motive. The judge's father brought a portable office building to town and placed it on a vacant Main Street lot that belonged to my cousin. He worked from that location for the next few years publishing a small newspaper to give his weekly comments and judgment on the corruption of local politicians.

I stopped giving him free help when his cattle scattered. Now the lady who manned the phones in the sheriff's office was frantic when she asked me to get his cattle off the highway. "You might cause a wreck! You might get someone killed."

My now furious cousin never fixed any significant part of our fence but must have vowed to make a malicious move at every opportunity for the rest of his life. The private road from my home and business to the public highway crossed a quarter-mile of his land. From time to time the county road crew helped with grading, gravel hauling, or snow removal. But he stopped that when he told the County Commissioners to "Keep your equipment off my land."

My customers complained about the rough access so I spent money that could have purchased more inventory and bought a small farm tractor and blade then made it top priority to smooth out the bumps every time the soil was wet enough to work. That piece of his land was once a cornfield bordered by thick willows. The spread of the willows could have been controlled by grazing hungry cows in the spring of the year. But through my uncle's lifetime he used it for a horse pasture. The willows kept getting thicker until it was impossible to ride a horse through them. It became out of the question to walk, see into them or get cattle out. The cousin tried burning. It caused them to come back thicker than ever. He borrowed a neighbor's tractor and brush cutter, only to ruin an engine when a stick knocked off an oil line. The only way to get cattle out of the brush was to bait them with flakes of hay behind an open corral gate.

One night I got a call from the Sheriff's office. "Are you burning something out there?"

Between my home and town the sky was a bright red, glowing from grown cottonwood trees exploding in a crown fire. A normal prevailing wind would have doomed my place but that night it was still with a slight breeze out of the north. Two local fire departments brought it under control.

A state policeman led me around the edge of the thicket, pointing out numerous places where the fire had started. He showed me ashes of several small fires that had been kindled in dry weeds. Most of them had made a spot the size of my hat and gone out.

I explained my cousin's motives and history and how he'd enjoy giving me a scare or feel no remorse if he burned everything I owned. The fire was controlled before I suffered any damage. The cop didn't want to open a "What if" can of worms or get involved with a scene where someone was told they couldn't burn trash on their own property. There was no further investigation and no charges were filed.

Over twenty years passed in which I had to tolerate a neighbor who despised me. I could only hope time would heal his wounds. His ranches totally surrounded the property where I live and ran my business. He also controlled the land on the north, the south, and part of the west of my other ranch on the Tularosa Creek. From his front door he could watch the floods coming down one big canyon or he could walk out to his barn and look down on the river. But he remained indifferent to the problems. I was faced with the choice of keeping up all the fences or being completely overrun when his stock came visiting. His coin machine business fell apart in his divorce case. My retail trade boomed and then dwindled away when we decided to retire. Health problems that came with advancing years took their toll on each of us. His was a heart attack, surgery and severe limits on his physical activity. I had the advantage of being some fifteen years younger but arthritis, a plastic hip joint and fast-approaching seventieth birthday put an end to my ability to wear hip boots and splice barbed wire in a flooded stream.

The U. S. Forest Service took a dim view of letting cattle stray across fences. They issued maps with red markings to designate each rancher's maintenance responsibility. In their arsenal of weapons they also had monetary fines, reductions in permitted numbers and the threat of confiscation of livestock if they found them in the wrong place.

Forty years passed that they couldn't get my cousin to do his part, so without consulting me they inked a new map that gave me maintenance that had been assigned to him. They also decided to exclude everyone's cattle from the riparian areas along streams to protect some habitat for endangered species.

Going down the Negrito Creek there was a situation where a cow that crossed into the pasture my cousin refused to maintain had less than a mile to follow the stream and she would enter a piece of this holy land everyone was forbidden to use.

Then a quarter-mile later there was a block of private land, owned by a Tucson lawyer whose wife readily admitted she didn't have the physical strength to build fence. If my cattle failed to respect her "No Trespassing" signs she had no qualms about calling the Forest Service. This set the stage for them to give me threatening calls that my cattle were "...not where they're supposed to be." Dozens of trigger happy assistant rangers were sitting in offices or driving their green pickups up and down the roads watching for minor infractions to build trespass cases. This is how they climbed over each other to get their next promotion and pay raise.

It could all be applied to bring more pressure on me to fix more fences.

Glen stayed around home until his calves were sold each fall. Most ranchers found time for maintenance work during the winter but as soon as he got his check he towed a camper trailer to a warmer climate. Though he was not on my list of friends I continued to fix the fence and put his cattle back where they belonged.

My wife and I decided we owed it to ourselves to take a few vacations. I craved the chance to burn fuel on some road other than the one to Albuquerque. We wanted to spend time with our grandkids but any moment away from home was inviting theft on a grand scale. Many customers wouldn't pay if they could get it free. Everyone in the county knew we had thousands of dollars in merchandise in buildings that could be broken into in a moment. Outdoor items like steel posts, cinder blocks or welding steel weren't even protected by lock or key. We'd suffered so much petty theft during business hours we considered it unsafe to be gone overnight. It was risky to leave an hour for church or to eat a meal in town. Anyone could see where our car was parked and know how much time they had.

The best solution was a padlock on a gate where our road left the highway. But this point was an entry to my cousins' land, though a road he hardly ever used.

On one occasion his voice on my answering machine told me, "That damn thing ain't supposed to be locked." I sent a key to him and another to Shawn Menges, the County Sheriff, who had a part time job helping take care of those cattle. Several months later, long after I thought the problem was solved, Shawn told me, "He refused to accept that key. He insists that gate isn't supposed to be locked."

More time passed. I had no intention of making any move that affected my cousins' property rights but thought it was my duty to protect my own. I thought he'd have the decency to discuss any problem face to face.

The time came that it was my cattle, running from town dogs that crossed the fence into his pasture. It was two days before we were to leave to take a couple of our grandkids to Mt. Rushmore. There was no way to know how many days would pass before those cattle would go into his corral for a bait of hay. But it would give him an opportunity to reciprocate for all the times I'd taken care of his when he wasn't home. His son, Ricky, was now sharing the work. I gave him a key and told him, "I hope you and I can get along better than your Dad and I." All was in perfect harmony.

The next morning Ricky phoned to tell me he had caught two yearlings in the pen. My cousin stood on the outside of the corral while

156

I loaded them into my trailer. I told him I'd given Ricky a key. Again there was no hint of disagreement.

He reciprocated a few days later. We were two thousand miles away in South Dakota when we got calls telling us the lock and chain had been cut off the gate, leaving it open for anyone to enter. We'd left people watching our place who provided their own lock and chain until we returned. They got a deputy sheriff to investigate and they assured us this cousin was doing all he could to continue the feud into the next generation. He'd sent his teen-aged grandson, Cody, to give us the word, "If you lock it again we'll cut that too."

On our way home we met with a young lawyer in the District Attorney's office to see if the breaking and entering constituted a criminal case. He dismissed us with the judgment that a lock and chain was inconsequential property damage, only a petty misdemeanor and they couldn't be bothered.

Glen must have wanted to leave some evidence he went through the gate to fix fence. Fifty feet that I had kept low across an elk trail were now standing tall. It was an invitation for the next herd to destroy it. Holes remained on both sides of where he worked. There was a broken wire where my heifers had fled from the dogs and a fallen cottonwood limb that had also damaged the fence.

Within a few months Quentin, a different grandson entered the scene—assigned the duty of keeping hunters and trespassers off the property. I didn't condone some damage this land was getting from trail bikes and all-terrain-vehicles but found it interesting to count the steel posts they used—ten along my short driveway—to put up "No Trespassing" or "No Hunting" signs. He never spent the price of a single post to help me maintain the fences.

The chance that a hunter might set foot on their place infuriated Quentin to the point he started closing my gate and turning back my customers during the daytime. I had to lock open the same gate on which they had cut a chain when I wanted it closed.

They targeted Grem Lee, a talented and friendly young artist who was badly crippled by multiple sclerosis. All the rest of the community treated Grem with compassion and helped him in any way they could. He enjoyed his time outdoors but his only remaining method of mobility was on a four-wheel ATV. I encouraged him to drive around my gate when he found it closed. Now a four foot strip of weeds and willows became so valuable they had to exclude a man who couldn't walk. Quentin drove a post and posted a "No Trespassing" sign in the middle of Grem's ATV trail.

We learned there is no exemption from someone who chooses to use or abuse you. No amount of good works or neighborly acts can change one who refuses to change. But I'll go to my day of judgment saying I did more to help him than he helped me.

Chain cut off metal gate.

Top: Steel post in bike trail. Bottom: Blocking bike trail. This cousin never contributed a new post to fence maintenance but used seven along my quarter-mile driveway to deter off-road bikers.

Weeds and willows so valuable he had to exclude a man who couldn't walk.

Chapter Seventeen

FIGHTING IN CHURCH

Trouble always found me. Though I tried to do the right thing, trouble always came my way. My efforts at helping people often made someone mad and they blew up in my face without warning. The first chapter of this book described the animosity that built up in one church congregation while I was helping them construct their building. My route of escape came when a different group put up their building and welcomed me and my family. We spent over thirty years attending and worshiping in relative harmony with the rest of the congregation. Shorty Winfield, the preacher who started that church was never idle and always had time to give encouragement. He worked through the week as a carpenter. He could dish out spiritual guidance from the top of a ladder while waiting for his helper to cut the next board. He and his wife grew a big garden so a handful of surplus squash became his ticket to getting some people to let him inside their door. The Winfield's helpful ways and friendly attitudes soon packed this new church with people. A church in Ruidoso, NM, took the lead in collecting support money from several other churches, sent it here to construct the building and paid his salary. But the time came that the Winfields moved on to other challenges and Ruidoso told us we had to stand on our own feet. Things turned downhill from the moment the Winfield's left. Many of those who had been attending died, lost interest or moved away.

When Ruidoso cut off their support we had a preacher with a young family living in a nearly new mobile home. They had to go somewhere he could make a living so we took over the payments and paid off the dwelling. Now we had a nice church building, a good place for a preacher to live and very few people to make use of it.

We went through several arrangements in which someone came in and gave a message on Sunday. It satisfied the ones who would attend anyway but it was doing nothing to attract new members. We needed someone who would get acquainted with the whole community, know each person's weakness and problems and go to the place of need instead of waiting for someone to come to them. Years passed with my name and phone number published in the classified ads of a monthly church newspaper letting its readers know we were looking for a preacher. It yielded an occasional phone call, gave us our first contact with two of the preachers who did us no good, and brought in an infrequent visiting minister.

My own Bible knowledge never went deep enough to qualify me to lead any lessons or ask the proper questions to qualify a preacher. The only ones we could afford were men who already had some pension or retirement check. With high hopes of success I helped bring in one from Colorado. He was a Hispanic, which made me think he would be a good fit for the community. He had two teen-aged kids which I assumed would give him a head start on getting young people involved. His method of presenting himself as available to the community was an answering machine telling people to leave a number to call if anyone wanted to study. Then his kids drug him down when the cops arrested them several times for drinking and drug parties.

The funds we could offer from what appeared on our collection plate promised slow starvation. Other churches pledged assistance then someone forgot to write the check.

Next we brought in a young preacher from South Dakota who waited until he got moved in to tell us he was allergic to the smell of cigarettes. Smoking was becoming illegal in public places but enough people were still sneaking a discreet puff around the cafes and public gatherings to make him hide in a hole all week, just coming out to give a lesson on Sunday. About the time he moved on, some argument blew apart a church in Springerville, Arizona. Two families quit attending there and joined our group. It looked like their loss was to be our gain. One couple got out of bed early enough on winter mornings to travel a hundred miles with a tiny baby. I'd never seen such dedication. They led songs, Bible study lessons and left generous contributions on the collection plate; our bank account grew rapidly which they said would help attract a preacher.

Their method of study, however, gave me real problems trying to stay awake. Relying heavily on cross-referencing from their Concordance they spent the morning in hopscotch from book to book and verse to verse trying to show the relationship of one part of the Bible to another. I stayed bored trying to stumble through the reading of names no one could pronounce and waiting while each person found the correct place. Everyone was using a different version or translation.

Each told the same thing but with a different choice of words, making it difficult to listen to the person in the next pew and know if we were all on the same topic. If we stayed with it we might gain a deeper understanding but it was not the quality of study that would attract or hold new members. We were getting a Biblical history lesson with nothing to guide us through our daily problems.

One man brought his ten-year-old son, expected him to be absolutely still and quiet through two hours of tedious adult study and scolded him for every wiggle or chirp.

I wanted to attract young people, not drive them away.

These men's leadership gave them a top dog position. They started telling us what we were going to do. We had a tradition of bringing covered dishes and staging a pot luck dinner each time we had a visiting preacher. It was food and fellowship—the best part of a Sunday. Suddenly they stopped that practice and told me, "We'll take him to dinner at a café. That packed us into a crowded and noisy scene with a room full of boisterous elk hunters. Seating was scattered, service was slow, and visiting or discussion of church business impossible.

There were more deaths, more people moved away and our congregation dwindled until there were only two of us attending who lived in the community. The other local was Earl Pitt, dedicated and faithful but almost ninety years of age. He was nearly deaf and had multiple health problems. A family of three— a husband, wife, and her brother— retired from jobs in Arizona and moved to a place some twenty-five miles away in Luna, NM. They soon became active in their attendance and support.

Thelma and I had to handle the church business, keep the books, decide who received charity and hope the others approved. The building is heated with wood-burning stoves. I willingly cut firewood and built fires. It was use of one talent at which I was proficient. There was no one else to do that chore. The others would freeze when I couldn't attend. I became desperate, wanting to attract new members and felt the only way to make that happen would be with an active resident preacher living here and working in the town.

My years of running a store had built a barrier. People who had gotten their feelings hurt when I let them know they hadn't paid their bill weren't going to associate themselves with me in any group. My presence in any of the other churches could be disruptive and my understanding of their doctrines led me to believe they had departed a long way from the teachings of the Bible. I was left with no place to go if our doors ever closed.

We anchored to a pier of strength and leadership in Tom and Beth Collins who lived thirty miles away in Alpine, Arizona. He led worship from time to time and she taught classes for the children when any attended. They also spread the word that we were looking for a preacher and made contact with Lar Doyle, in Dallas, Texas, who offered to help us. At Tommy's urging I made several phone calls to Mr. Doyle. Tommy and I became convinced we may have found what we were looking for but we bumped into a wall of indifference when we mentioned his qualifications to the rest of the Arizona group. They told me, "Take it slow. Make sure he is the right one." Another time their advice was, "If you get the wrong one, he'll tear up the church when you have to get rid of him." They grilled me with dozens of questions about every thing from Mr. Doyle's personal life to his answers on questions about how to interpret unexplained portions of the Bible.

With my own mistakes and limitations fresh in my mind from questions I hadn't asked when we hired other preachers, I gave them copies of Mr. Doyle's resume and urged them to make their own calls. They brushed me off with the claim the two-hour time difference between Texas and Arizona didn't give them any time at the end of their work day.

I took it upon myself to offer Mr. Doyle some help with his travel expenses if he would come here, get his feet on the ground in our community and see if he thought he could work with us. It would be a two-way appraisal; each of our group could form their own opinion. Mr. Doyle was frugal. He put the trip off to save mileage and scheduled our visit to coincide with some stop he wanted to make in West Texas.

My mind wandered when I was in church. I'd look out the window and watch the small kids ride their bikes in the street. Teenagers roared around on motorcycles, hot-rod cars or all terrain vehicles. There were times their noise drowned out our services. If Bill

Lytle or Shorty Winfield were still in town they would know each young person by name and find a productive use for that energy. They would get them to haul trash or bake cookies and teach them a Bible verse while they were at it. Could we get another man here who would provide their level of leadership or would our doors soon be locked for lack of interest?

I wanted to grab those kids and bring them in. The younger ones were passing through a time of their lives when we could have a positive influence. We might plant seeds that would lay dormant through the inevitable rambunctious latter teen stage, then sprout and be productive when the time came to raise their own families. If we didn't use this chance the opportunity may never again come their way.

Mr. Doyle came to check us out, gave a Sunday lesson and joined us for a pot-luck dinner. This was the time for the face-to-face meeting, a one-on-one visit and the chance to ask any questions. One of our Arizona members didn't bring his wife and bailed out the door within seconds of the end of the closing prayer. I managed to catch up with him before he got across the parking lot. Decisions might be made before the day was over and I wanted everyone's input.

"Well I don't know. It's nothing, but I'm not familiar with the translation he used." He drove away, without giving me further direction. The next time he came to church he brought two pages of computer printout regarding mistakes that could be found in the New International Version of the Bible.

His partner told me, "There dozens of translations and they all have mistakes. There are no exact English words to always get the same meaning as was written in the original Greek and Hebrew."

Then the first man came back waving a Bible that was printed in English and Greek, side by side on the same page. He held it high in the air and yelled, "I want the truth!"

I considered it no more than a stage prop if it was in the hands of anyone who couldn't read Greek.

Calls to Mr. Doyle showed he considered the argument irrelevant and told me he would use any version that was easy to understand. He gave me further encouragement to hire him when I asked him what price we'd have to offer him. His answer was, "That's not important. Make me an offer." We went through that routine several times and his answer was always the same. He also told me to take my time. "I'm in no hurry."

Tom Collins and I both thought we should nail him down before he got away. The others stalled, asking, "Have you phoned the references he gave on his resume?" Then they negated any benefit to such a call by saying, "He wouldn't give us a name of anyone who wouldn't give him a good report." He had given us four names and phone numbers which I divided among the group with each person to contact one of them.

A week went by. We all talked to answering machines or received recordings for discontinued numbers. No one had talked to a live person and the members who had held reservations now voiced outright opposition, "That's bad! His hand-picked references won't support him."

Mr. Doyle sent a new list of references. I talked to two and got very strong and enthusiastic endorsements. "He'll do you a good job." Another man told me, "I'd sure hate to see you get him. We don't want to let him go from here."

Tom and Beth Collins also checked references and got good reports. There were good reasons for the return calls we couldn't get. Some had moved and one was out of the country.

Day by day, call by call Tom and I were becoming more convinced we were moving in the right direction. Those two who wouldn't ring a phone weren't supporting us and wouldn't tell us why, but their caution progressed into direct opposition.

Mr. Doyle told me, "Get each of your group to write me about two simple sentences—nothing elaborate. I want to know what each of you expects of me.''

I answered, "I'll phone each of them and try to have it ready to mail next Sunday."
I've never managed to steer any group to go in the same direction. Each individual is going to be determined to do things his own way. Those two had concerns they weren't willing to share with me. "What's his address? I'll mail it myself."

The next Sunday I boldly announced. "I don't need two sentences. I told him my expectations with two words. 'Be available.'" But the notes I could mail that showed our support were disappointing. One man brought me a written note as I'd asked. Another stalled with, "I'm still trying to think of the right thing to say." Then there was, "I wrote it but I didn't have any stamps to mail it." One lady who I thought I could count upon for help said, "I didn't get your message. Something must have gone wrong with my answering machine."

Doyle's response after those notes got to him was, "There are about ten people associated with your church. I won't go there unless I have the support of more than half. I haven't received six notes from members who really want me. I want to know where I stand. Write me a letter that answers these three questions. How much will you pay me? Which translations of the Bible am I not to use? How many of you want me? Pass something around and get everyone to sign it.''

I thought they were all legitimate questions we should answer, so I drafted a letter which should address our problems while offending no one.

Fully aware that people could quickly become explosive in questions regarding their religion I got Thelma to send e-mail copies to everyone so they could comment or make changes. For those who couldn't receive e-mail, I read it word for word over the phone.

My offer on a price was my own suggestion, fishing in the dark; it was a figure that was sustainable with what was being left on the collection plate.

No one called with any comment but I found myself in front of a hostile audience the next Sunday. Some thought I'd offered him too much money, others not enough. One lady voiced legitimate concern about signing anything. She said, "That means he can look around the room and point to any of us and say, "You wanted me," or "You didn't want me."

One of our Arizona members gave no explanation, but stormed "No. I'm not about to sign it." He called Tommy Collins out into the parking lot and there was a conversation that was not meant for me to hear.

RESERVE CHURCH OF CHRIST
PO BOX 228
RESERVE, NEW MEXICO 87830

November 15, 2009

Dear Lar:

We need your leadership in the church at Reserve, NM. We have nice facilities that were put here through the generosity, dedication, and hard work of members, friends, and other churches in the past. Death, health problems and move-aways have reduced local participation to only a few. Three very unselfish families from Arizona are currently driving long distances and expending an enormous effort to lead our services. If it were not for their energy our doors would be closed. But they have their obligations to their jobs and their communities. Two and a half hours on Sunday mornings are all that we are open.

We need local resident leadership for our church to be any asset to our community. That is someone who will circulate among the people at the ballgames and in the coffee shops, get acquainted with them and learn their needs and problems. Empathy with someone who is sick or hungry can be the key to uncovering spiritual needs.

We can offer you $1,000.00 per month plus the partly furnished mobile home. We'll also pay for electricity, water, sewer, propane, and firewood. Any additional attendance should bring a good chance of more contributions. Other churches who have helped us in the past may be willing to help again, so we should be able, within time, to offer you more. We'll also pay the expenses for a moving van to get your personal belongings to our town.

Some members have concerns about complete and accurate translations of the Bible and have requested the Revised Standard Version not be used.

We hope this meets your approval and we can continue to look forward to getting you here working with us.

Sincerely,

Earl W. Ribb - 89 yrs.

Thelma McCarty
Bobbie Durham
Rose Thomas (Rosemary Finch 81)
Norma Jean Emerson

The letter.

When Lar Doyle visited us he had spent some time briefing us on his personal history, including a messy divorce when his wife left him to live with other men. He made the honest confession, "There were times I was mad enough to kill her."

Now our men who were looking for reasons not to hire him distorted this to say, "He stood right there in that pulpit and advocated killing his wife."

168

Obviously out-numbered and out-voted I told them "You are closing the door on this church, but "I've given it my best shot. I feel like a whipped dog, sneaking away with his tail tucked between his legs." Then I said, "There is no reason for me to stay if we're not doing something to be an asset to the community."

The situation worsened when Tommy, Beth, and I went to a café for lunch. He asked me, "Where do we go from here?" That conversation in the parking lot had been to tell him neither of the other Arizona members would be back. This blow up had taken away our leadership and the cash flow I was counting on to keep things going. Their reaction would have been appropriate if I'd advocated converting the building into a brothel or a casino, but I was trying to bring a preacher to fill a vacant pulpit in an empty church.

Tommy agreed to continue leading the lessons. We had no song leader. I wrote a letter to Mr. Doyle, thanking him for his interest but admitting I'd failed to get more than half the group to support him.

Tommy didn't give up. He got Mr. Doyle on the phone and they decided it wouldn't be necessary for everyone to sign something. With those two dissenters out of the picture he wouldn't be moving into direct opposition. They'd left us with enough money to keep him on the job two years. Maybe in that time we could build up the attendance to keep things going. We were gambling he would bring the personality and ability to be successful.

A few months later I gained deeper insight into what drove his opposition. Edwin Carlisle had preached and conducted meetings at our church. Then for a time he was the preacher for the church in Springerville, Arizona. We all had complete confidence in his leadership.

Carlisle's wife passed away while he was at Springerville and he married a widow from our congregation, then they moved to property he owned in Texas. As far as I can learn this was before the dissatisfaction entered the Springerville group that caused two of their families to come to ours.

Next Rosemary Finch, our staunchest, most faithful and hardest working member developed cancer and moved to Seattle, Washington to be near two of her daughters during treatment. There was nothing the medical community could offer that helped for long and she endured two years of agony in hospitals and a nursing home before passing on to her reward.

This was in December, about the same time as Tommy Collins persuaded Lar Doyle to take our job.

Rosemary's daughters planned cremation then a memorial service in our town the following March. They contacted me for help finding space to make beds for a large extended family. I offered them the four bedrooms and two bathrooms we weren't using in our preacher's trailer. I thought, if Mr. Doyle got moved here by then he would be satisfied with one of the bedrooms and let them have the other three. The trailer also had a living room and a den with two couches that could make temporary bedroom space for quite a crowd.

Mr. Doyle had to give his landlord thirty days notice before leaving. Then he scheduled extensive dental work. Next he decided to remain out of the way until the Finch family was through with the trailer. The result was that the plans we thought would happen in December were postponed into late April. The Finch girls arranged for Edwin Carlisle to come here from Texas to conduct their mother's service.

Meanwhile my doctors, in January, scheduled me for a hip replacement surgery in the middle of March. It worked out to be two days before the Finch service. Edwin Carlisle got started conducting the service, collapsed and had to be taken to the hospital by ambulance. Everyone who witnessed it thought he had a heart attack but the medical diagnosis blamed it on some problem with his nerves. The end result was that he and I were assigned bedrooms two doors apart in the hospital.

I stirred a hornet's nest when we tried discussing church business. He steadfastly claimed there was no authentic Bible except the King James Bible. I'd been taught it used too much obsolete language and almost any of the others were easier to understand. He staunchly defended those who had left our group because they thought we were introducing something that was impure. When I argued that we had to either bring in new leadership and recruit new members or close the door he said, "Be patient, pray about it. The Lord works in mysterious ways. He will take care of you."

170

If this was to be the focus of church I was in the wrong place. Those kids playing in the street needed to learn the Ten Commandments. These were lessons they could get from any Bible. I'd rather they'd get them in understandable English with no "Thee" or "Thou" thrown in. They needed basic education in what was right and wrong. The deep analysis or teachings of the Minor Prophets and how they foretold the coming of the Savior was wasted effort that would go over their heads.

We had no way to look into the future and know what success Lar Doyle or anyone else in that pulpit would bring. But a church without a congregation is an empty building. Without active leadership we were heading in that direction.

I'll close this work as I opened it. Someone has to roll up his sleeves and go to work. I remember a time a different preacher was telling me it wasn't his job to work at construction and if the Lord wanted him to have a church he would provide it. I was just a half-trained carpenter, father of three small kids who needed some Bible training, and I carried a trivial smattering of some sense of right and wrong. For some reason my destiny was to spend my life trying to help people who became mad at me at every turn.

The years I'd spent trying to save a failing ranch were now obviously wasted. I left a record of this struggle in my first book, *Trouble in a Green Pickup*. The community had failed to accept the store I'd put here for their convenience, and now the church I'd tried so hard to save was apt to soon be unused and vacant.

Maybe I will get high marks for my effort when I cross that Last Divide. At least I'd get there knowing that there is truth in the lessons that I was never put here to please man.

I hope my record will show I tried to make proper use of the talents I was given. If I were to be one of the soldiers who were lost in battle I would hope it would be known that I went all the way thinking I was trying to do what was right.

THE END

Thelma and me. (Photo by Marnie Ashby)

Building and running the store was a joint effort as is typing, revising and updating through two books. Thelma's hobbies are oil painting and making quilts. She hates to read and write but she has helped me every time I've asked for fifty years.

ABOUT THE ARTIST

Both the cover illustration and the cartoon on page 64 were drawn by Grem Lee, who is also the illustrator of *New Mexico Magazine's* "Ol' Slim's Views from the Porch." Lee, 48, has been drawing ever since he could hold a pencil. He was raised on horseback at the Y Ranch in the rough-and-rocky country of southwestern New Mexico. He is a cowboy, a hunter and a hunting guide himself. Also known by Navajos as the crazy white man — *bilaga'ana diigis.*

Grem continues to draw despite having the crippling disease of MS (multiple sclerosis) ... or BS as his family and friends say.

Today the outlaw might be found somewhere in the same desolate Gila Mountains that Geronimo once prowled. *Quien sabe*?